The KNITTER'S BOOK *of* FINISHING TECHNIQUES

NANCIE M. WISEMAN

Martingale™
& COMPANY

The Knitter's Book of Finishing Techniques
© 2002 by Nancie M. Wiseman

Martingale & Company
20205 144th Avenue NE
Woodinville, WA 98072-8478
www.martingale-pub.com

Printed in China
12 11 10 09 08 07   15 14 13 12 11 10 9

Library of Congress Cataloging-in-Publication Data
Wiseman, Nancie
    The knitter's book of finishing techniques / Nancie Wiseman.
        p.   cm.
    ISBN 1-56477-452-X
    1. Knitting.   I. Title.
    TT820 .W62 2002
    746.43'2—dc21
                                          2002007725

MISSION STATEMENT

We are dedicated to providing quality products and service by working together to inspire creativity and to enrich the lives we touch.

CREDITS

PRESIDENT: *Nancy J. Martin*
CEO: *Daniel J. Martin*
PUBLISHER: *Jane Hamada*
EDITORIAL DIRECTOR: *Mary V. Green*
MANAGING EDITOR: *Tina Cook*
TECHNICAL EDITOR: *Ursula Reikes*
COPY EDITOR: *Karen Koll*
DESIGN DIRECTOR: *Stan Green*
ILLUSTRATOR: *Robin Strobel*
COVER AND TEXT DESIGNER: *Trina Stahl*
PHOTOGRAPHER: *Brent Kane*

DEDICATION

I'D LIKE to dedicate this book to all of you who knit and have questions, but no one to get the answers from. I hope this book will answer most, if not all, of your questions about knitting and finishing techniques. It was a pleasure for me to write and I hope you'll find it a pleasure to read and use. I hope all your knitting turns out beautifully and your finishing is perfect from now on.

ACKNOWLEDGMENTS

A VERY special thank-you to Ursula Reikes, my editor and friend. You make the work easy and fun. I appreciate all of your comments and suggestions. Thanks to the folks at Martingale & Company for publishing this most enjoyable book to research and write. I applaud your efforts to make every book you publish better than the last. You are all a joy to work with.

I would like to give special recognition to Robin Strobel, the graphic artist at Martingale & Company who did all of the wonderful illustrations for this book. Thank you for your time, patience, and willingness to learn and ask questions about knitting so the artwork is always perfect. Chocolate for everyone!

Thank you to Cascade Yarns for providing all of the yarn used in the book. Your generosity is very much appreciated.

And to my husband, Bill, once again, I can't thank you enough for taking such good care of me. Thanks for cooking, running the errands, and walking the dogs so I have more time to knit and write. You are my special treasure, and I hold you closest to my heart.

CONTENTS

INTRODUCTION

*T*HE TECHNIQUES in this book will give you everything you need to finish your knitted garments perfectly. Many of them can be found in other books, but here you'll find an explanation of the benefits and the drawbacks of each technique, in addition to how to work it. Most of the techniques are referenced for knitted sweaters, but you'll find that many of them also apply to afghans, scarves, or any other knitted item. It doesn't matter whether you are a continental knitter or an American (English) knitter; the techniques are the same.

Doing the preliminary work of finding the right cast on, increase, decrease, and cast off will make your knitting more enjoyable and the finished garment a joy to wear. You might also want to explore some of the techniques in the book that you have never used.

At the back of the book is a worksheet that you can photocopy to help you plan your sweater; on it you can record what cast-on and cast-off shaping and seams you will be using. Read through the techniques, find the one(s) that fit your needs, and fill in the blanks on the worksheet. This is also a good place to keep track of rows and make any notes necessary.

If you plan your finishing before you start the garment, all edges will have the same selvage—if a selvage is used—and all bands will be worked with the same method. You'll be thrilled to see how much better your garments go together when you plan in advance for the finished product.

NANCIE'S FINISHING SECRETS

- Leave long ends when you cast on, so you can later use them for seaming. Never trim an end until you're sure you're not going to use it somewhere for a seam.
- If you absolutely hate finishing, don't wait until all the pieces are knit to start. When the body is done, work the shoulder seams and the front or neck bands before you start the sleeves. It will let you begin to see what the finished product is going to look like. Small rewards in small steps bring instant gratification and success.
- Make your swatches large enough, at least 8 inches square, so that you can use them to experiment with finishing techniques such as picking up stitches or to decide the type of band you want to work at garment edges. Be sure to bind off your swatches and keep them. You can also carry them with you when looking for buttons if needed.
- If you always work all of your finishing in the same order, you'll know exactly where to go to find the ends if you ever have to rip part of the garment out for some reason.
- Steam and moisture are your best friends for blocking. Don't be afraid to use them.
- If you've had to work with a stitch or two over and over to get a technique correct, and the yarn is wool or a wool blend, drop some water on the stitch when done to shrink it back up. In general, when the stitches are knit over and over they stretch out and look very loose.
- When you discover an error in a stitch pattern a few rows back in your knitting and you think that it will be okay, or that no one will notice it, don't leave it. You're probably going to wish you had ripped it out the further away you get from it. Go back and fix when you find it. You'll never like the sweater if you don't.

CAST ONS

*Y*OU HAVE to start your knitting in some way, and casting on is the way to get stitches on your knitting needle. There are so many techniques for casting on that sometimes it is hard to choose the right one for the project at hand. The following cast-on (CO) techniques are the best known and most popular methods. They are all useful, but not all in the same way. You must consider where to use them and the final effect they will have on the finished item. If you choose wisely, you should always be satisfied with the way your cast-on edges look.

When casting on for knit one, purl one ribbing, cast on an even number of stitches. On the wrong side, work (purl one, knit one) to the last two stitches, purl two. On the right side, knit two, (purl one, knit one) to the end. This gives you a one-knit-stitch seam allowance at both ends of the ribbing. Weave the seam one stitch in at both ends for a perfect seam and no interruption in the rib pattern. (See "Seams in Ribbing," page 66.)

For knit two, purl two ribbing, cast on a multiple of four stitches plus two extras. On the wrong side, work purl one, (knit two, purl two) across, end purl one. On the right side, knit one, work the knit two, purl two ribbing across the row, and end with knit one. Continue rib in established pattern. Weave the seam one stitch in at both ends for a perfect seam and no interruption in the rib pattern. (See "Seams in Ribbing," page 66.)

NOTE: *The slipknot counts as a stitch when working any of the cast-on techniques except the tubular or provisional cast on where the slip knot is part of the crochet chain.*

Long Tail Cast On

This is the most common and versatile cast on used by knitters. The result is a nice-looking edge if the cast-on row is used as the right side and the first row worked is a wrong-side row. For a bind off with a similar look, see "Traditional Bind Off" on page 50.

L to R: Long Tail or Slingshot Method Cast On with Garter Stitch, Stockinette Stitch, and Ribbing

Benefits

♦   Can be used to start virtually any knitting project.

♦   Easy to execute, but tension must be controlled.

♦   Two ways to work cast on: slingshot method and thumb method.

♦   Works well with all weights of yarn.

Drawbacks

♦   Requires long enough tail to work the cast on; if you run out you have to start over.

♦   Correct placement of the yarn in your fingers is essential.

♦   Easy to work this cast on too tightly.

♦   Cast-on edge, followed by stockinette stitch, will not lie flat; it will roll toward the knit side.

To Work

For both of the methods described below, measure out the tail estimating about 1" for each stitch you will be making plus about 12" extra for tails. This is a rough estimate: with bulky yarn this might not be quite enough; with fingering yarn it might be a bit too much.

Slingshot method: Make a slipknot and place the loop on the right needle. You can use two needles held together in your right hand to make this cast on looser. They don't have to be the same size; the ribbing needle and a smaller needle will work well. Or you can use the larger needle called for in the pattern to work the cast on, but don't forget to change back to the smaller needle to work the ribbing.

Hold the tail and the working yarn with your left hand out and across from the right hand holding the knitting needle. Hold the slipknot on the right needle with your right index finger. Insert your left thumb and left index finger between the two pieces of yarn *from the top*. Separate the yarns, and rotate your left hand up with your fingers toward the sky. You'll notice that a loop formed on your thumb. *Using the needle in your right hand, go under the loop of yarn on the left thumb and then over the yarn on your left index finger and bring that yarn through the loop. Let go of the yarns and tighten gently, but do not pull too tight. Repeat from * for the number of stitches needed.

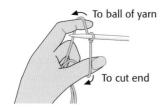
To ball of yarn
To cut end

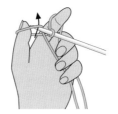

Thumb method: Make a slipknot and place the loop on the right needle, leaving a long tail. Wind the tail end around your left thumb, front to back. Wrap the yarn from the ball over your right index finger and hold it tightly in your hand. *Insert the needle upward through the loop on your thumb. Using your right index finger, wrap the yarn from the ball over the needle as if knitting a stitch. Pull the yarn through the loop on your thumb to form a stitch and drop the loop off the left needle. Tighten the loop on the right needle by pulling on the tail end. Repeat from * for the number of stitches needed.

To cut end   To ball of yarn

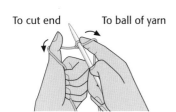

KNITTED-ON CAST ON

THIS IS a very common cast on because it feels like normal knitting. It varies just slightly from the cable cast on (page 14) but the effect is quite different. The looser edge created at the bottom sometimes gets slightly distorted near the edges where the seams are put together. The traditional bind off is the best match (see page 50).

L to R: Knitted Cast On with Garter Stitch, Stockinette Stitch, and Ribbing

Benefits

♦ Easy to remember.

♦ Can be used to start any project, or to add stitches with knitting in progress.

♦ Fairly elastic; size of stitches can be controlled easily.

♦ Works well with all weights of yarn.

♦ Both sides look exactly the same, so it doesn't matter what row you work first when beginning to knit.

Drawbacks

♦ Can stretch out of shape easily if done too loosely.

♦ First row of knitting will look loose and appear to have holes. Knit into the back of the stitches (on the first row worked after cast on only) to tighten them up and close the holes.

♦ Cast-on edge tends to be loose and can snag easily or pull out of shape. Cast on with a smaller needle to eliminate this problem.

♦ Cast-on edge, followed by stockinette stitch, will not lie flat; it will roll toward the knit side.

To Work

Make a slipknot and place on left knitting needle. *Knit into the stitch on the left needle as you normally would *without dropping the stitch off the left needle.* Place the new stitch from the right needle onto the left needle, holding needles point to point. Remove the right needle and repeat from * for desired number of stitches.

Knit into stitch.

Place new stitch on left needle.

TIP: *Enlarge the loop of the new stitch to make it easier to place on left needle. Pull gently until stitch is normal size, keeping tension on all stitches the same.*

CABLE CAST ON

THE EDGE of this cast on will always look and remain very firm. The first row worked after the cast on is a right-side row. For matching bind off, see "Traditional Bind Off," page 50.

L to R: Cable Cast On with Garter Stitch, Stockinette Stitch, and Ribbing

Benefits

+ Can be used for casting on stitches with work in progress.
+ Can be used for some buttonholes.
+ Works well with dense stitch patterns that don't have much stretch.
+ Creates an edge with a neat and uniform appearance when executed with even tension.
+ Works well with all weights of yarn.
+ Can be used for all cast-on edges; be careful not to work too tightly.

Drawbacks

+ Cast on is not very elastic; tends to be firm and dense, but that may be desirable.
+ Easy to work cast on too tightly.
+ Edge of cast on will be tight, but the stitches on the needle will appear loose. Knit into back of stitch to tighten on next row.
+ Cast-on edge, followed by stockinette stitch, will not lie flat; it will roll toward the knit side.

To Work

Make a slipknot and place on left needle. Knit into the stitch and place result-ing stitch on left needle by inserting the left needle into the stitch from the right side of the loop, or by your right thumb, without dropping stitch off left needle. (See "Knitted-On Cast On," page 12.) *Insert right needle between two stitches on left needle, wrap yarn around the needle as if to knit, pull the new loop through to the front, place the new stitch on the left needle as directed above. Do not drop any stitches off the left needle. Repeat from * for desired number of stitches. When working the first row, if the cast-on stitches look loose, knit into the back of each stitch to tighten them up.

Insert needle between two
stitches. Knit a stitch.

Place new stitch
on left needle.

TIP: *Enlarge the loop of the new stitch to make it easier to place on left needle. Pull gently until stitch is normal size, keeping tension on all stitches the same.*

PICOT CAST ON

A ONE-STITCH picot will make the cast on very elastic, but will show only slightly. Making a picot with more than one stitch will leave a larger loop that can be charming on baby items, on a collar, or on the top of a sock if the picots are close together. Separate the picots with more stitches between them to prevent a ruffled edge. When used with matching picot bind off (See "Picot Bind Off" on page 58), all edges will have the same elasticity and look.

L to R: Small Picot Cast On with Garter Stitch, Stockinette Stitch, and Ribbing

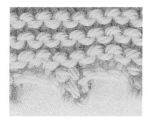

L to R: Large Picot Cast On with Garter Stitch, Stockinette Stitch, and Ribbing

Benefits

- ◆ Cast-on edge is elastic.
- ◆ Decorative, yet useful.
- ◆ Works well with ribbing or garter stitch.
- ◆ Picots can vary in size from one stitch to many stitches. The more stitches, the larger the loop of the picot.
- ◆ Can be easily adapted to change number of stitches between picots.
- ◆ Either side can be used as right side.
- ◆ Works best with light- to medium-weight yarns.

Drawbacks

◆ Picots placed close together can cause the cast-on edge to ruffle.

◆ Cast on must be worked evenly and firmly for uniformity, using a needle two sizes smaller than the needle you're going to use next.

◆ The loops formed by the picots might get caught on sharp objects if made too large.

◆ Should not be worked on bulky yarns because the picots will be too large and cause the cast-on edge to flare or ruffle.

◆ Cast-on edge followed by stockinette stitch will not lie flat; it will roll toward the knit side.

◆ Takes more than usual amount of time.

◆ Takes more than usual amount of yarn.

To Work

For small picots: Cast on three stitches using cable cast on (see page 14), *knit two stitches, bind off one stitch (one small picot made), place remaining stitch on right needle back on left needle as if to purl. Cast on two stitches using cable cast on. Repeat from * for half the number of stitches needed for the cast on. Next row: **Knit first stitch on needle, pick up the loop on top of the picot using the left needle from back to front, purl the new stitch through the front of the loop. Repeat from **, end knit one. Begin pattern or ribbing on next row.

Cast on three stitches. Insert needle for first knit stitch.

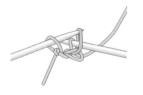

Knit two stitches. Bind off one stitch.

Pick up loop on top of picot. Purl new stitch.

For larger picots: Cast on four stitches using cable cast on (see page 14), *knit two stitches, bind off one, knit one stitch, bind off one (large picot made), place remaining stitch on right needle back on left needle as if to purl. Cast on six stitches, repeat from * for desired number of stitches, end by placing remaining stitch on right needle back on left needle. Begin pattern or ribbing on next row.

CHAINED CAST ON

THIS TECHNIQUE is generally used to create a temporary cast on; see "Tubular Cast On" (page 20) or Provisional Cast On" (page 24). If left in, it will result in a firm edge. If the chain is to be removed, as in the provisional cast on, the loose stitches that remain must be placed on a knitting needle to keep them from unraveling. A border of some sort can then be added; work in the opposite direction of the knitting.

If you are using the chain cast on as a simple edge, begin pattern or ribbing after cast on is complete. If the cast on is worked in the main yarn followed by stockinette stitch, the edge will not lie flat. The edge will require a border, such as single crochet or an I-cord edge to keep it from rolling to the knit side of the work. The first row is the right side of the knitting.

L to R: Chained Cast On with Garter Stitch, Stockinette Stitch, and Ribbing

NOTE: *Whenever you are instructed to use "waste yarn" for a cast on, use a light-to medium-weight cotton yarn because the cotton yarn will not leave little flecks of color behind when you remove it. When the chain is finished, cut yarn and finish off. Tie a knot in the tail so you know from which end to remove the chain.*

Benefits

- Best used as the start of the tubular cast on and the provisional cast on.
- Works well with all weights of yarn.
- Easier than crocheting a separate chain and then picking up stitches into the back of the chain, as usually recommended when this technique is used.

Drawbacks

♦ Removal of chain must be done carefully.

♦ Cast-on edge, followed by stockinette stitch, will not lie flat; it will roll toward the knit side.

♦ Takes more time.

To Work

Use the required needle size, appropriate yarn (waste yarn if the chain is to be removed, or the actual knitting yarn if it is to stay in), and a crochet hook similar in size to the knitting needles. Make a slipknot in the yarn and place on the crochet hook. *Hold the needle and yarn in the left hand, and the crochet hook with the slipknot in the right hand as though crocheting. Place the needle on top of the yarn held in the left hand. Holding the hook over the needle, crochet a chain stitch over the top of the knitting needle. Move the yarn under the knitting needle and back toward the left. Repeat from * for desired number of stitches.

Crochet a chain over top of knitting needle.

Cut the yarn, remove the loop from the crochet hook and pull the yarn through it. Tie a knot in the end of this tail so you know from which end to remove the chain.

TUBULAR CAST ON

THIS TECHNIQUE leaves beautiful cast-on edges. The extra elasticity of the cast on makes the garment fit better. It is wonderful for sweaters that fall at the hip, where the cast on needs to be loose so as not to hug the body. Using this cast on and the Kitchener stitch bind off (see page 54) results in the most professional-looking cast on and bind off you can use.

L to R: Tubular Cast On with Garter Stitch, Stockinette Stitch, and Ribbing

Benefits
♦ Rounded edge resembles edge found on designer garments.
♦ Very elastic edge, perfect for ribbing at the hips.
♦ Can be used to start any knitted piece using knit one, purl one ribbing.
♦ Works well with all yarn weights except bulky.

Drawbacks
♦ Takes more than usual amount of time.
♦ Works best with knit one, purl one ribbing, but can be used with stockinette stitch and other stitch patterns.
♦ Does not work well with bulky yarns; makes edge too thick, and causes it to flare out.
♦ Will always end with an odd number of stitches, meaning there will be a knit stitch at both ends with the right side facing you.

To Work

With needle size required for ribbing, and cotton yarn in a contrasting color, work chained cast on (see page 18) for half the number of required stitches, plus one. With the main color yarn, knit one row, purl one row, knit one row. With the purl side facing, *purl first stitch on knitting needle, insert the right needle from top to bottom under purl bar of *main color* buried in the contrasting color yarn three rows below. Place this stitch on the left needle by inserting the needle from front to back into the stitch, and knit the stitch in the front of the loop.

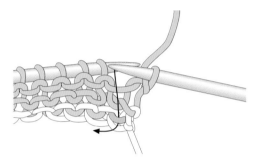

Pick up next stitch from loop in contrasting yarn.

Repeat from *, end with purl one and no loop to pick up for another knit stitch. On next row, work knit one, purl one ribbing as established (this is considered the first row). Or work desired pattern on first row. If your pattern requires an even number of stitches, you can make up for the loss of the stitch after the ribbing is completed by working an increase.

After the first row is completed, you can remove the chain. Unravel the chain starting at the end with the knot (see "Note," page 18). You will have to

pick out the chain for a stitch or two, but then it should be easy to rip out. By easy I mean it will pull out slowly and will not need to be cut. If the chain does not rip out easily and you must cut it to remove it, then you made an error in making the chain or in picking up the knit stitches from below the chain. The cast on will not hold together if you have to cut the chain somewhere in the cast on to remove it. You will have to work the cast on again to correct the error. It's better to realize there is a problem now, before you've knit the whole piece.

You will notice that as you pull the chain out, one of the strands of the contrasting yarn will remain in the middle of the "tube" of the cast on. If you'd like to put knitting elastic through this tube, tie the elastic to the end of the crochet chain that does not have the knot and gently pull it through as you remove the chain. This is a good idea if this cast on is used with cotton yarn, as the ribbings in cotton tend to stretch out.

White chain is partially removed. Double strand of red elastic at bottom will be pulled through as chain is removed.

Tubular Cast On with Knit One, Purl One Ribbing

If you research this technique further, you will find directions for working the tubular cast on for knit two, purl two ribbing as well. I am never pleased with the finished look when I've used this technique so I prefer not to use it; therefore I don't recommend it. Also, the matching bind off to the knit two, purl two cast on does not leave as smooth an edge as it does for knit one, purl one.

PROVISIONAL CAST ON

PROVISIONAL CAST on works well if you want to work your borders after the sweater is knit. This may be because you aren't sure what type of border you want to use or you're not sure you have enough yarn for all borders to be the same. It is often easier for people to work a looser bind off than cast on, so this allows all of the borders to be bound-off borders so they match. It also allows you to control or make adjustments in the way the border fits. When you are putting the sweater together, you won't notice whether everything was knit in the same direction or not.

L to R: Provisional Cast On with Garter Stitch, Stockinette Stitch, and Ribbing

Benefits
♦ Can be used when you want to add a contrasting rib or border later, to work an I-cord border, or to remove the cast on and pick up the stitches to work in the opposite direction.
♦ Can also be used for a firm edge if it is done in the main color of yarn and is not removed.
♦ Works well with all weights of yarn.

Drawbacks
♦ Leaves you one stitch short when the chain is removed.
♦ Leaves more than usual amount of ends to weave in.
♦ Takes more than usual amount of time.

To Work

With needle size required for body, work the chained cast on (see page 18) for the number of stitches required for body after the ribbing is completed. Begin with the right-side row of the pattern above the ribbing. Remove the chain when the piece is finished. You can remove the chain after a few rows of knitting, but you must place the stitches on a stitch holder or knitting needle until you are ready to knit them.

To remove the chain, unravel the crochet chain from the end with the knot while placing each stitch on the needle. Be careful to remove one chain at a time, so the knitting doesn't unravel. Begin border, keeping in mind that if you were to increase above the ribbing according to the pattern, you would now decrease to the desired number of stitches and work the ribbing in the opposite direction. See the worksheet on page 140 for calculating evenly spaced decreases. Bind off loosely.

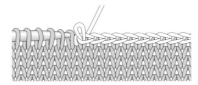

Remove chain one stitch at a time.

Alternative Method to Work Chained Cast On

Using waste yarn, crochet a loose chain of the same number of stitches needed for cast on plus a few extras. Finish off, cut yarn, and tie a knot in the yarn so you know from which end the chain should be removed. Turn the chain over, insert the right knitting needle into the loop on the back of the chain, and knit on a stitch. Repeat for as many stitches as needed. If the chain becomes too tight, skip a chain if necessary. This will not ruin the cast on. It is not necessary to redo the cast on if the chain is distorted because you picked up the wrong thread. It will need to be cut out when removed, not gently ripped out.

Knit on stitches in the
back of the chain.

Front of Chain After Stitches
Have Been Picked Up

INCREASES

*I*NCREASES, ALONG with decreases, are instrumental in knitting to create shape, texture, and design. Combining increases and decreases using a specific plan or pattern can result in stitches knit on the bias, or stitches that look lacy, or like they are moving across the surface of the knitting. There are various ways to do both. Increases will be covered first.

Most knitting patterns will not tell you what type of increase to use; the direction will just say "increase." But choosing the right increase and using it throughout your work will make your knitting look more even and consistent. In some cases, the increase you choose will help you with the finishing of the piece as well.

Below, you'll find the three most common ways to work increases. When you are required to make increases at both ends of the same row they should be worked to mirror each other, so that both edges will look the same after seaming. That's why it's important to know about right-facing and left-facing increases. If for example you were to use the same make-one increase along both edges, the stitches along the seams would look different after seaming.

Increases for shaping should be worked at consistent intervals. For example, every right-side row, or every fourth row. This will help you keep track of them, and it may also add a decorative look to the edge, depending on the increase you choose.

One dilemma with increases is when you are instructed to increase evenly over a certain number of stitches. In some cases it is a guessing game, or you end up doing it a couple of times to get it right. See the worksheet on page 140 to help you calculate the placement.

KNIT IN FRONT AND BACK
OF A STITCH OR BAR INCREASE

THIS INCREASE is easy to execute and can be used anywhere in a knitting project. However, the increase does create a little "bar" that will show on the knit side. When worked from the knit side, the bar will always be to the left of the stitch the increase is made from. Worked on the purl side, the bar will be on the right of the stitch used to make the increase when you look at it on the knit side.

At the beginning of a row, you can work the increase on the first or second stitch, depending on whether you want one or two stitches before the bar. At the end of the row, make the increase on the second stitch from the end for one stitch to remain, or on the third stitch from the end for two stitches to remain. Be sure to leave the same number of stitches at each end so that both edges will look the same.

If you are working in a knit and purl pattern, use a knit stitch to create the increase. If you are working the increase in the middle of the work to create a symmetrical design, make the first increase on the first stitch to the right of center and then again on the center stitch.

When worked in the body of the garment, the increase will not have any effect on seaming or picking up stitches. Working this increase one or two stitches from the edge of a garment will leave at least a one-stitch seam allowance, which will make seaming and/or picking up stitches easier.

Increases at Left and Right Edge Worked Every Other Row

Increases at Left and Right Edge Worked Every Other Row in Garter Stitch. Yellow yarn shows increases, which are invisible.

Benefits

+ Can be used virtually anywhere in a knitted project and on both the knit and purl side of the work.
+ Helps you match up rows when used for sleeve increases; the bar created by the increase will match on the two edges of the seam.
+ Virtually invisible when used in a knit and purl pattern, especially when worked between a knit stitch and a purl stitch in ribbing.
+ Works with all weights of yarn.

Drawbacks

+ "Bar" created by the increase shows on the right side of the work.
+ Requires a stitch to make the increase, so it cannot be substituted for an increase that does not require a stitch. (See "Make One Increase (M1)," page 30.)
+ Requires special care to keep "bar" within same column if increases are worked on knit and purl side.

To Work

On the knit side: Knit into the designated stitch on the left needle, but do not drop the stitch off the left needle. Move the right needle toward the back of the work, knit into the back of the same stitch. Drop the old stitch off the left needle, creating two stitches from one stitch.

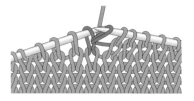

Knit into stitch but do not
drop it off left needle.

Knit into back of same stitch.

Increase in Purl on Purl Side

Increase in Knit on Knit Side

On the purl side: Purl into the designated stitch on the left needle, but do not drop the stitch off the left needle. Move the right needle toward the back of the work, insert it into the back of the stitch from left to right, and purl again. Drop the old stitch off the left needle.

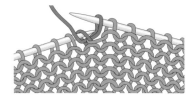

Purl into stitch but do not
drop it off left needle.

Purl into back of same stitch.

MAKE ONE INCREASE (M1)

THIS INCREASE is considered one of the most invisible increases available to knitters. It must be worked between two stitches. When used one stitch in from the edge it will leave a one-stitch seam allowance that will make seaming or picking up stitches easier. Because it is virtually invisible, it will barely be seen if used anywhere within the work. It can be used in pattern stitches as well, but cannot replace a "knit in front and back of stitch" increase if you are directed to use that increase.

Left Cross Make One on Left Edge

Right Cross Make One on Right Edge

Benefits

- ◆ Creates an invisible increase.
- ◆ Does not involve another stitch, but must be made between two stitches.
- ◆ Two versions of this increase, one that slants to the right and one that slants to the left, are mirror images of each other.
- ◆ Can be used virtually anywhere as well as on either the knit or the purl side of the work.
- ◆ Works with all weights of yarn.

Drawbacks

- ◆ Must be worked between two stitches.
- ◆ Must be worked carefully so that a hole is not formed where increase is made.
- ◆ Requires extra attention to make sure right- and left-slanting versions of increase are made at correct end of needle.
- ◆ When used row above row, it will not be as invisible, and may pucker the edge. Preferably worked on every other row or further apart.

To Work

NOTE: *The "running thread" between two stitches that is used to make this increase is really a yarn over that didn't get enlarged by wrapping the yarn around the right needle in the previous row. If you knit this running yarn incorrectly, it will create a hole that looks just like a yarn over.*

Right cross make one: Used at the beginning of the row. On the knit (or purl) side: Locate the running thread that connects the stitch just worked and the stitch to be worked on the left needle. Insert the left knitting needle from back to front under the running yarn. Knit (or purl) into the front of the stitch to twist it closed.

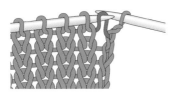

Insert left needle from back to front through "running thread."

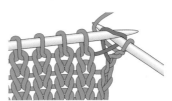

Knit into front of stitch.

Left cross make one: Used at the end of the row. On the knit (or purl) side: Locate the running thread that connects the stitch just worked and the stitch to be worked on the left needle. Insert the left knitting needle from front to back under the running thread. Knit (or purl) into the back of the stitch to twist it closed.

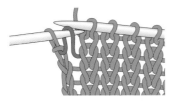

Insert left needle from front to back through "running thread."

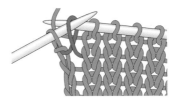

Knit into back of stitch.

If either method results in a hole, remove the new stitch and work again. Hole will occur if running thread was picked up wrong or wrong side was knit.

RAISED INCREASE

THIS IS an invisible increase that can be worked on both knit and purl sides. When used along the edges, this increase should be worked after the first stitch knit at the beginning of the row, or one stitch before the last stitch at the end of the row. This will leave a stitch along the edge for the seam allowance.

Left Raised Increase on Left Edge

Right Raised Increase on Right Edge

Benefits

- ♦ Good all-purpose increase for both the knit and purl side.
- ♦ Very invisible.
- ♦ Works well for multiple increases across a row.
- ♦ Easy to work and remember the right-slanting and left-slanting versions.
- ♦ Good increase to use if you have made an error in your stitch count and need to add a stitch invisibly somewhere in the knitting.

Drawbacks

- ♦ Cannot be used in the same column of stitches row after row; must have a row of knit or purl between the increases. Will pucker edge of knitting if worked every row.
- ♦ More difficult to work on purl side because the area used to create the increase is harder to see.

To Work

Right raised increase (used at beginning of row): Work to the stitch where the placement of the increase will be on the right side of the stitch. Insert the right needle, from front to back, into the right edge of the knit stitch from the row below, being careful not to pick up two strands of yarn. Knit the stitch from the row below, then knit the next stitch on the needle. On the purl side, work in a similar manner using the right side of the purl bar from the previous row, except purl the stitch from the row below, then purl the next stitch on the needle.

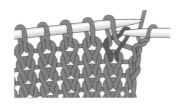

Left raised increase (used at end of row): Work to and including the stitch where the placement of the increase will fall on the left side of the last stitch knit. Insert the left needle, from front to back, into the left edge of the last knit stitch from the row below, being careful not to pick up two strands of yarn. Knit the stitch from the row below and continue across. On the purl side, work in a similar manner using the left side of the purl bar from the previous row, except purl the stitch from the row below, then purl the next stitch on the needle.

DECREASES

IMPLY STATED, decreases are made by working two stitches together. There are several ways to work decreases, and when they are worked at both ends of the same row they should be worked to mirror each other. For example, if you work the same decrease on the right and the left side of a neck opening, one side will look neat and tidy and the other side will look like it has extra yarn crossing over the stitches used for the decrease.

The various decreases in this chapter will be shown as pairs, one slanting right and one slanting left. Learning the various decreases is one thing, but knowing which one to use where is the other important part of using the different decreases. Decreases worked one or two stitches in from the edge are called "full fashion" decreases and are a bit decorative. Decreases worked at the very beginning and end of the row won't show, but they make seaming and picking up stitches more difficult.

When a decrease of two stitches must occur up the center of a design, these decreases don't slant left or right; they go straight up the center of the knitting. These "central decreases" are generally used to shape motifs, or for decorative purposes.

Decreases are given for the knit and purl side of the work. Although the decrease will only show on the knit side, you need to be able to work a matching decrease on the purl side and the knit side in case decreases are worked on every row, or on purl rows.

As with increases, there are times when you must decrease a certain number of stitches across a row. See the worksheet on page 140 to help you calculate the placement.

Knit Two Together (K2tog) and Purl Two Together (P2tog)

This is the most common decrease known in knitting. It is simple to work and easy to remember. It is a right-slanting decrease, which means it slants to the right into the knitting. This decrease is worked at the end of the row. At the beginning of the rows, work its mirror-image (see "Slip, Slip, Knit [SSK] and Slip, Slip, Purl [SSP]" on page 37) left-slanting decreases.

Knit Two Together on Left Edge with Two-Stitch Seam Allowance

Generally these decreases are worked one stitch in from each end. This leaves a very easy area to see and work with when picking up stitches, if needed, or when working seams. To make the decreases with a one-stitch seam allowance at the end of the row, work to three stitches from the end, work decrease, finish the row. It is worked the same whether it is a purl row or a knit row. More stitches can be left after the decrease if desired for a more decorative effect.

Benefits

♦ Worked at end of rows.
♦ Works with all weights of yarn.
♦ Good decrease to use when told to work many decreases across a row.
♦ Acts as a right-slanting mirror-image decrease to left-slanting slip, slip, knit, or slip, slip, purl (see page 37).

Drawbacks

♦ If at least one stitch is not left after decrease on the edge of the work, it is very difficult to seam or pick up stitches.
♦ Shows only on knit side whether worked on the knit side or purl side.

To Work

Knit two together (K2tog): Knit to the stitches to be decreased, insert the right knitting needle into the first two stitches on the left knitting needle as if to knit, wrap the yarn around the right needle in the normal manner, and knit the two stitches together. Drop the two stitches just knit together off the left needle.

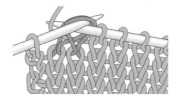

Knit two together.

Purl two together (P2tog): Purl to the stitches to be decreased, insert the right knitting needle into the first two stitches on the left knitting needle as if to purl, wrap the yarn around the right needle in the normal manner, and purl the two stitches together. Drop the two stitches just purled together off the left needle.

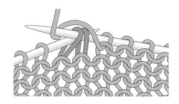

Purl two together.

SLIP, SLIP, KNIT (SSK)
AND SLIP, SLIP, PURL (SSP)

SLIP, SLIP, KNIT or slip, slip, purl, when used as the mirror image of knit two together or purl two together, will make the "row" with multiple decreases on the left and the right sides of the garment look exactly the same. This decrease will show on the right side only. If worked on every other row, the result will be a nice line at the neckline or sleeve opening that will make seaming or picking up stitches easier. There should be a one-stitch (or more if desired) seam allowance left before or after the decrease. Be sure both edges match.

Slip, Slip, Knit on Right Edge with Two-Stitch Seam Allowance

Benefits

- Acts as a left-slanting mirror-image decrease to right-slanting decrease, knit two together or purl two together (see page 35).
- Worked at the beginning of rows.
- Works with all weights of yarn.
- Replaces slip one stitch, knit one stitch, pass the slipped stitch over (S1, K1, PSSO) for a neater decrease.

Drawbacks

- More difficult to remember than knit two together or purl two together.
- Takes a little more time than knit two together or purl two together.
- If at least one stitch is not left before decrease on the edge of the work, it is very difficult to seam or pick up stitches.

To Work

Slip, slip, knit: On the knit side, slip two stitches, one at a time, as if to knit. Insert the left needle from left to right into the front of the two stitches and knit the two together from that position. Drop the two stitches just knit together off the left needle.

Slip two stitches to right needle.

Knit two stitches together.

Slip, slip, purl: On the purl side, slip two stitches, one at a time, as if to knit. Transfer the stitches back to the left needle. Insert the right needle from left to right through the back of the stitches and purl the two together from that position. Drop the two stitches just purled together off the left needle.

Move two slipped stitches
to left needle.

right

Insert right needle through back
of stitches and purl together.

With Wrong Side of Work Facing: L: Purl Two Together Worked at End of Row. R: Slip, Slip, Purl Worked at Beginning of Row. Decrease does not show on wrong side.

CENTRAL CHAIN DECREASE (CCD)

THIS IS a decorative decrease worked with a stitch to the right and a stitch to the left of a center stitch.

The decrease incorporates three stitches into one, leaving a raised row of knitting. When worked across a row with corresponding increases, it leaves a decorative zigzag border.

Central Chain Decrease Worked up the Center

Benefits
♦ Purpose of decrease is to leave a central stitch and decrease a stitch from both sides of it.
♦ Used for motif shaping.
♦ Makes a zigzag pattern in knitting when used in combination with yarn overs or other increases.
♦ Worked on every other row, on the knit side.
♦ Works with all weights of yarn.
♦ Works with most stitch patterns.

Drawbacks
♦ The central stitch will not be as obvious in garter stitch, unless it is purled on the wrong side.
♦ Depending on the weight of the yarn used, can leave a very thick row of knitting where stitches sit on top of each other.
♦ Pulls up the sides of the knitting, creating a diamond shape if worked by itself; there will not be a straight edge at bottom of knitting.

To Work

Worked on knit side only: Knit to one stitch before the center stitch where decrease is to be located. *Slip the next two stitches together as if to knit from the left needle to the right needle: that is, the one stitch before center and the center stitch. Knit the next stitch, pass the two slipped stitches over together. Continue across the row.

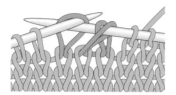
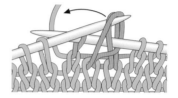

Slip two stitches together as
if to knit. Knit next stitch
on left needle.

Pass two slipped stitches over
knit stitch on right needle.

To keep the decrease in a straight line on subsequent rows, work to one stitch before the central stitch of the decrease and repeat from * above. Your stitch count should be reduced by one stitch on each side of the center stitch. If necessary, mark the central stitch with a pin to help you find it.

Double Central Decrease
(Sl 1, K2tog, psso)

Like the central chain decrease, this decrease incorporates three stitches into one, but the result is a flat row of knitting with stitches crossed over each other. It is worked in the same position as central chain decrease (see page 39), but the effect is completely different.

Double Central Decrease Worked up the Center

Benefits

♦ Purpose of decrease is to leave a central stitch and decrease a stitch from both sides of it.

♦ Makes a zigzag pattern in knitting when used in combination with yarn overs or other increases.

♦ Used as a decorative decrease.

♦ Flatter than central chain decrease, without a raised stitch.

♦ Used for motif shaping.

♦ Worked every other row on right side.

♦ Works with all weights of yarn.

Drawbacks

♦ Not as smooth-looking as central chain decrease, but flatter.

♦ Pulls up the sides of the knitting, creating a diamond shape if worked by itself; there will not be a straight edge at bottom of knitting.

To Work

Worked on knit side only: Knit to one stitch before the center stitch where decrease is to be located. *Slip the next stitch as if to knit from the left needle to the right needle: this is the stitch before the center stitch. Knit the next 2 stitches together, the center stitch and the stitch after it, pass the slipped stitch over. Continue across the row.

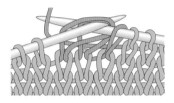 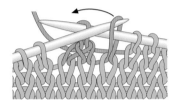

Slip one stitch as if to knit.
Knit next two stitches together.

Pass slipped stitch over the knit
stitch on right needle.

To keep the decrease in a straight line on subsequent rows, work to one stitch before the central stitch of the decrease and repeat from * above. Your stitch count should be reduced by one stitch on each side of the center stitch. If necessary, mark the central stitch with a pin to help you find it.

SELVAGES

ELVAGE STITCHES, also known as seam allowances, are not always necessary when knitting. In fact, if they are never used, the seams of the garment will still look fine, especially on a garment without body shaping. But there are times when using a selvage stitch will make the seams look even better, such as on edges with increases and decreases. The seams will also be easier to sew.

One of the reasons selvage stitches are used is to prevent stockinette-stitch edges from rolling toward the purl side. This edge rolls because the purl bars across the wrong side of the work are shorter than the Vs of the knit stitch on the right side of the work; the work rolls to the side with the shorter stitch. Many of these selvage stitches, depending on how many stitches are used, will prevent the edges from rolling, but narrow selvages won't completely stop them.

There are two basic selvage edges that are popular, and you either love them or you hate them. One is the slip stitch selvage and the other is the garter stitch selvage. I generally don't use selvage stitches except in ribbing and in garments with pattern stitches where the continuity of the pattern would be lost if one stitch on each edge was used for the seam. For example, if you were to use a basket-weave pattern of knit four, purl four, and did not use a selvage stitch, you would lose one stitch from the edge of both pieces when you sewed the seam. The pattern would then look like knit three, purl three at the side seam (see "Seams in Pattern," page 67).

In plain stockinette stitch, you don't need to use a selvage stitch because there is no pattern to ruin when you sew the seam. Some knitters prefer to make a selvage stitch to help with seaming later. Leaving one or more stitches before and after decreases or increases is essential for picking up stitches later, or for sewing seams.

SLIP STITCH AT BEGINNING OF EVERY ROW

THIS SELVAGE stitch can help with seaming and with reducing bulk at the seams. Do not work this selvage stitch on edges where stitches will be picked up later because it can leave holes. Also, if you use this selvage stitch on edges, the ratio for picking up stitches will change. (See "Picking Up Stitches," page 86.) If used on the edge of garter stitch, as on a scarf, the little chain created up the side is a charming addition.

Stockinette Stitch with Chain up the Edge

Garter Stitch with Chain up the Edge

Garter Stitch with Tighter Knot at Edge

TIP: *When you are instructed to slip a stitch knitwise or purlwise, it does not mean that you move the yarn to the knit or purl position before you slip the stitch. If the yarn is to be moved before the slip stitch, the instructions will tell you. Slipping the stitch knitwise or purlwise is used to place the stitch on the right needle in a certain position.*

Benefits

- ♦ Has three versions.
- ♦ Leaves an enlarged chain up the edge of the work, one chain for every two rows, which can help you count rows.
- ♦ Helps with sewing seams together.
- ♦ Leaves a beautiful edge when used with garter stitch.
- ♦ All increases or decreases should be worked inside selvage stitch.
- ♦ Works well with all weights of yarn.

Drawbacks

- ◆ Easy to forget if you don't use this technique all the time. It will show if part of a seam has the slip stitch and part of the seam does not.
- ◆ Reduces bulk when used for seams, but can leave the seam looking a bit loose.
- ◆ Requires two different methods, one for garter stitch and one for stockinette stitch.

To Work

For stockinette stitch with chain up the edge: Slip the first stitch of every knit row knitwise with yarn in back. Slip the first stitch of every purl row purlwise with yarn in front.

Slip stitch knitwise with yarn in back.

For garter stitch with chain up the edge: Slip the first stitch of every row purlwise with yarn in front, move the yarn to the back, and knit across the row.

Slip stitch purlwise with yarn in front.

For garter stitch with tighter knot at edge: Slip the first stitch of every row knitwise with yarn in back.

Slip stitch knitwise with yarn in back.

Garter Stitch Selvages with Stockinette Stitch

This technique is perfect for achieving the same number of rows in corresponding pieces. It also helps with seaming because the knots at the edges will match perfectly, but it may require a bit more blocking to make the seam lie flat with less bulk. If you use two stitches as a selvage, you will need to add extra stitches to work the selvage stitches. Losing four stitches at each seam will reduce the size of the knitting too much.

The more stitches used for the selvage, the less the knitting will roll if stockinette stitch is between the selvages. This works very well when added to knitting with color work or with a stitch pattern that you don't want to interrupt with a seam. It can also help you keep track of what row you are on in the pattern or chart; each garter-stitch knot at the edge equals two rows.

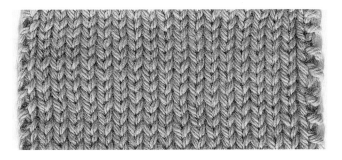

Garter Stitch Selvages

Benefits

+ Decorative selvage for pieces that won't have seams.
+ Any bulkiness it leaves in seams usually can be steamed and flattened out.
+ Helps slightly to control the roll at the edges of stockinette stitch.
+ Very elastic; helps control some patterns that grow in length due to the pattern stitch or to too slippery a yarn.
+ Fits to contours such as armhole shaping or neck shaping.
+ Helps the knitting lie flat.
+ Works well with pattern stitches that have a knit and purl pattern.
+ Works well with most weights of yarn; bulky yarn can be too thick for seaming.

Drawbacks

+ Slightly thicker seams.
+ Can leave a bulky selvage after picking up stitches. Can be used at neck or armhole edges, but leaves the seam allowance thick
+ Best not to use with bulky yarns if seams will be sewn.
+ If used on a piece, it must be used consistently, as the selvage where it is used will be shorter than the selvage where it is not used.
+ Easy to forget. Place markers before and after selvage stitches to help you remember.

To Work

For seamed edges: Knit the first one or two and last one or two stitches of every row.

DOUBLE SEED STITCH SELVAGE

THIS PATTERN requires a minimum of two stitches to work. If you use it in a seam, add extra stitches to work the selvage stitches, because if you do not, the pattern will reduce the size of the knitting too much. The more stitches used for the selvage, the less the knitting will roll if stockinette stitch is between the selvages.

Double Seed Stitch Selvages

Benefits

- Leaves a wide seam on pieces that need seaming.
- Leaves the seam a little bulky, but usually can be steamed and flattened out.
- Slightly flatter than garter stitch and less bulky.
- Decorative on pieces without seams.
- Helps control the roll at the edges of stockinette stitch.
- Works well with most weights of yarn (except bulky yarn).

Drawbacks

- Makes thick seams if worked with bulky yarn.
- Too wide to use where stitches will be picked up.
- If used on a piece, it must be used consistently, as the selvage where it is used will be shorter than the selvage where it is not used.
- Easy to forget, when it is two stitches wide. Place markers before and after selvage stitches to help you remember.

To Work

On every row: Knit one, purl one at the beginning of the row, and purl one, knit one at the end of the row.

BIND OFFS

*A*LSO REFERRED to as casting off, the purpose of binding off is to finish off stitches so they won't unravel. There are numerous places where you will need to bind off (BO) stitches, including at the end of a project and for buttonholes, neck shaping, and armhole shaping.

There are many techniques for binding off stitches. Some are decorative, some are just a way of ending off stitches, and some are both. Choosing the correct bind off is important for good finishing and smooth, clean edges that make finishing easier. Some bind-off techniques require knitting needles, some need a yarn needle with the knitting needles, and some require a third knitting needle. It is easy to work a bind off too tightly, so you must be careful to make the bind off as elastic as the knitting.

Here are some general pointers to help you bind off.

- To bind off loosely with the traditional bind off, always hold a needle in the right hand one to two sizes larger than the needle in the left hand. Do not tug on the yarn after each stitch is bound off. Maintain tension for entire edge. Pull out on the edge to be sure it is elastic.
- Always bind off in pattern when appropriate with the bind off you are using.
- Experiment with the different bind-off techniques when you work your swatch. It will help you decide which one you want to use.
- If you are not sure of the finishing technique you will be using for the bound-off edge, set aside on another needle until you have all pieces finished; you can make the decision then.
- After binding off, leave long tails that can be used in seams, so there are fewer ends to weave in.

TRADITIONAL BIND OFF

THIS TECHNIQUE yields a nice edge wherever it is used, as long as it is not worked too tightly. It can be used in virtually all areas that require bound-off stitches.

L to R: Traditional Bind Off above Garter Stitch, Stockinette Stitch, and Ribbing

Benefits

- The most commonly used bind off; also known as "pullover bind off."
- Easy to learn because it is "knitting" with a simple added step.
- Can be bound off in pattern stitch, whether knit or purl, right or wrong side.
- Works well with all yarn weights.
- Mirror image to long tail cast on (see page 10).

Drawbacks

- Easy to work too tightly; to help bind off loosely, use a needle one or two sizes larger in the right hand only, and do not tug on the working yarn after each stitch.
- Forms the last row of knitting as well as the cast-off edge; must work in stitch pattern.
- The last stitch bound off can look loose or sloppy. (To correct, see "To Clean Up Last Stitch" on facing page).

To Work

Work two stitches in pattern, *insert the left knitting needle under the second stitch on the right needle, pull it over the top of the first stitch, and drop it off the needle. Work one more stitch and repeat from * until one stitch remains on right needle.

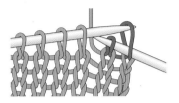

Pass first knitted stitch over
second stitch loosely.

To clean up last stitch: Bind off stitches until one stitch remains. Slip the last stitch to the right knitting needle. There are now two stitches on the right needle. With the left needle, pick up the left loop of the stitch below, return the slipped stitch back to the left needle, knit the two stitches together, and bind off.

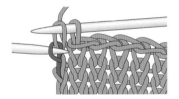

Slip last stitch to right needle. Pick
up left loop of stitch below.

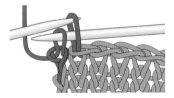

Return slipped stitch to left
needle and knit two stitches
together. Bind off.

To finish off last stitch: When there is one stitch left on the right needle, cut yarn and push through the loop of the last stitch and pull snugly to finish off.

To weave first and last stitch of circular bind off invisibly: After all stitches are bound off and finished off, cut the yarn leaving about a 10" tail, and thread onto a yarn needle. Insert the needle from front to back under the first bound-off stitch on the left that looks like a V lying on its side. Insert the yarn needle down through the center of the last bound-off stitch on the right. Weave the tail in on the wrong side.

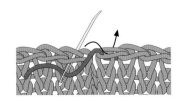

KNIT TWO TOGETHER BIND OFF

THIS TECHNIQUE leaves a firm, thick edge. It is not a good technique if a seam is to be worked at the bound-off edge. It is simple to execute, but can easily be done too tightly. It is generally used only in specific places (see "Benefits," below).

L to R: Knit Two Together Bind Off above Garter Stitch, Stockinette Stitch, and Ribbing

Benefits

- Sometimes used when binding off a partial row.
- Often used in lace to create a pointed edge.
- There is no "chain" on top of knitting as in traditional bind off.
- Works with light- to medium-weight yarns, too thick for bulky yarns.
- Good to use as the first row of a buttonhole, as it lies flatter than the traditional bind off.

Drawbacks

- Very specific use, not a general bind-off technique.
- Easy to work too tightly.
- Not appropriate for neck edges, shoulders, or armholes.
- Cannot be worked in pattern stitch.
- Bound-off stitches must be pulled out to the right as they are made so they are not too tight or bunched up.
- Has no matching cast on.

To Work

*Knit two stitches together. Place the resulting stitch, now on the right needle, back on the left needle as if to purl. Repeat from * across. Finish off.

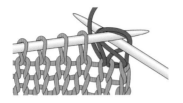

Knit two together.

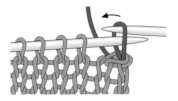

Place stitch back on left needle.

GRAFTING OR KITCHENER STITCH BIND OFF

USE THIS technique for neckbands or the front edges of a cardigan. It will give a very finished look to any garment when used in conjunction with tubular cast on (see page 20). It is worked in knit one, purl one ribbing.

Completed Bind Off

Benefits

♦ Very stretchy; predominantly used for bound-off stitches of a neckband to ease going over the head.

♦ Invisible; ribbing looks like a tube at the edge instead of like the straight line achieved with traditional bind off (see page 50).

♦ Can be worked flat or in the round.

♦ Works well with most weights of yarn; quite thick in bulky yarn.

♦ Perfect match to tubular cast on (see page 20).

Drawbacks

♦ Can only be used for knit one, purl one ribbing.

♦ Takes more than average amount of time.

♦ Bind off must be at the same tension as the stitches in the ribbing below.

♦ Requires extra double-pointed or circular needles and a yarn needle.

♦ Requires a lot of concentration, as it is easy to lose one's place.

To Work

Work knit one, purl one over an even number of stitches for desired length. Using two circular or double-pointed needles, depending on the number of stitches, separate the knit stitches from the purl stitches. As the stitches face you, (insert one needle into the first knit stitch, the second needle into the purl stitch) across. Half the stitches will be on one needle and half the stitches will be on the second needle. When you look at the knitting on either side, there will be knit stitches on the needle facing you.

Both pieces need to have the same number of stitches. Cut the working yarn about three times the width of the knitting plus about 12" extra to weave in. Thread yarn through a yarn needle. You will direct the yarn needle as if it were a knitting needle, working with the two pieces together, on knitting needles held in the left hand. Graft the stitches together as follows.

1. Go through first stitch on front needle as if to purl. Leave stitch on needle.
2. Go through first stitch on back needle as if to knit. Leave stitch on needle. Keep the yarn between the needles so it is not mistaken for another stitch. Adjust the tension as you work.
3. *Go through first stitch on front needle as if to knit, and through next stitch on needle as if to purl. Drop off first stitch on front needle.
4. Go through first stitch on back needle as if to purl, and through next stitch on needle as if to knit (see arrow in illustration below). Drop off first stitch on back needle*. Repeat from * to * until there is one stitch on each needle.
5. Go through remaining stitch on front needle as if to knit and drop stitch off.
6. Go through remaining stitch on back needle as if to purl and drop stitch off. Finish off by weaving in the end.

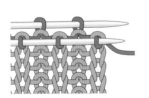
Place stitches on two needles.

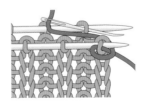
Steps 1 and 2

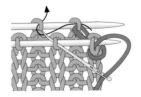
Steps 3 and 4

Two and Three Stitch I-Cord Bind Off, Also Known as Applied I-Cord

This technique leaves a nice rolled edge on the finished piece. If you need to seam the ends of the I-cord, graft the stitches together. (See "Grafting Live Stitches to Cast-On or Bound-Off Stitches," page 80.) If you are working around an edge like a collar or over a large number of stitches, you must work loosely, or the knitting below will be pulled too tight and pucker. Work with the same needles used for the body stitches or with a larger needle in the right hand if necessary to keep it loose. Do not over steam or block to flatten.

L to R: Two Stitch I-Cord Bind Off above Garter Stitch, Stockinette Stitch, and Ribbing

L to R: Three Stitch I-Cord Bind Off above Garter Stitch, Stockinette Stitch, and Ribbing

Benefits

♦ Rolled edge creates a nice finish to front edges, neck openings, button band, collars, sleeve bands, and pockets.

♦ Can be worked with either two or three stitches; two-stitch version leaves a very small edging; three-stitch version leaves a larger edge with more body.

Drawbacks

- Easy to work too tightly.
- I-cord seams require use of grafting or Kitchener stitch to keep the tube effect of the I-cord.
- Used over a long area, the rows below the bind off can pucker.
- Do not use on a seam that is going to be woven together, such as a shoulder seam.
- I-cord will not be uniform in size unless care is taken to pull the yarn tightly across the back of the I-cord when worked.
- Adding I-cord in a contrasting color to the main color of the knitting may result in a bit of the main color showing through. To prevent this, work the last row of main knitting (probably a purl row) in contrast color and then work I-cord in same color.
- Takes more than usual amount of time.
- Takes more than usual amount of yarn.

To Work

With completed knitting on the left needle, cast on to the left needle two stitches for two-stitch I-cord or three stitches for three-stitch I-cord, using cable cast on (see page 14). *Knit one (two) stitches, slip, slip, knit (see page 37) with last stitch of cast-on stitches and first stitch on left needle. Transfer the two (three) stitches back to the left needle as if to purl. Pull the yarn tightly across the back of the work and repeat from *.

NOTE: *The technique is the same if you are working on the purl side of the work.*

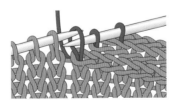

Three-Stitch I-Cord
Transfer three stitches back
to left needle as if to purl.

PICOT BIND OFF

THIS TECHNIQUE can be used on any edge that does not get seamed. It works well on baby clothes where lots of stretch is needed for neckbands or cuffs. It's a good idea to work the bind off with a size 2 or 3 needle to keep the picots as small as possible.

Sample Bound Off with Cast On One Stitch, Bind Off Three Stitches
L to R: Garter Stitch, Stockinette Stitch, and Ribbing

Sample Bound Off with Cast On Three Stitches, Bind Off Six Stitches
L to R: Garter Stitch, Stockinette Stitch, and Ribbing

Benefits

- Decorative edge as well as bind off.
- Used on edges that will not have seams.
- Number of stitches between picots and size of picots easy to change.
- Very elastic, good for neck edges.
- Works well with ribbing.
- One stitch in the picot leaves a moderate amount of elasticity; more stitches in the picot make the edge more elastic and the picot more visible.
- Makes a decorative edge on all garment borders when matched with picot cast on (see page 16).

Drawbacks

♦ Picots worked too close to each other can cause the edge to ripple, which may or may not be desirable.

♦ Loops on picots can get caught on sharp objects or small fingers.

♦ Takes more than usual amount of time.

♦ Takes more than usual amount of yarn.

To Work

To add elasticity to the bound-off edge without the picots being very visible: *Cast on one stitch using cable cast on (see page 14), bind off three stitches using the traditional bind off (see page 50), place remaining stitch on right needle back on left needle as if to purl and proceed from *.

To make the picots more decorative and larger: Work as above, but **cast on from two to four stitches, bind off double the amount you cast on. Proceed from ** using the numbers you have chosen. To separate the picots even more, bind off more stitches between the cast-on stitches.

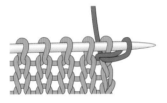

Cast on one stitch using
cable cast on.

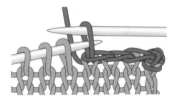

Bind off three stitches, then slip
stitch on right needle to left needle.

SEAMS

$\mathcal{E}$VEN A beautifully knit garment will look awful if the seams are done poorly. It's the make-or-break point for most knitters. There are a variety of options for sewing seams, as well as a variety of seams to be sewn. The woven seam is the seam of choice in most cases, but there are other options such as knitting seams together and grafting seams together.

In general, you should work the seams with the same yarn as was used in the knitted pieces. If the yarn is too thick or has bumps or slubs, you can use another yarn in the same color and preferably in the same fiber content. Embroidery floss and needlepoint wool are good alternate choices for joining seams. They both come in an array of colors, so it is usually easy to match them to the knitting. If you have knit the garment in a heavyweight yarn, you could use a lighter weight yarn in the same color to weave the seams.

Use yarn needles, not tapestry needles, to sew your seams. Tapestry needles are sharp and can split the yarn. Yarn needles are dull, have a large eye for the yarn to go through, and will go under stitches instead of through them. You will find that working at a table instead of in your lap usually makes the stitching and tension more even. The finished seam should have as much stretch as the rest of the knitting.

If you have always hated finishing, one of the reasons is probably that you've spent hours on it, worked very hard, and then when all was said and done, you weren't happy with the way the finishing looked. Once you learn to work seams correctly and get beautiful results, I don't think you'll hate finishing any more. It takes time and patience. It's a good idea to spend some time practicing with swatches or small sweaters.

When putting a garment together, this is the general order to follow.

- ♦ Block the pieces to the correct measurements (see page 134).
- ♦ Sew on pockets and work any embellishment.
- ♦ Sew or knit together shoulder seams.
- ♦ Work any front, neck, and/or buttonhole bands before the sleeves are sewn in so the piece is not so big to work with.
- ♦ Sew sleeves to armholes.
- ♦ Sew side seam of body from cast-on edge to armhole.
- ♦ For a vest, work armbands.
- ♦ Sew sleeve seam from cast-on edge to armhole.
- ♦ Weave in all ends
- ♦ Block again if necessary.

STARTING YARN FOR SEAMING AT CAST-ON EDGE

Using tail from cast on: With yarn on yarn needle, right side of knitting facing, and tail coming from the piece on the right, *insert the needle from back to front into the edge of the cast on of the knitting on the left. Make a figure eight with the yarn, and come back under the edge of the cast on for the piece of knitting on the right. If the tail is coming from the left, work in reverse. Begin seam.*

Using new piece of yarn: With yarn on yarn needle, and right sides of knitting facing, insert the needle from back to front above the cast-on edge of the piece on the right. Leave a long enough tail to weave in later. Follow from * to * above.

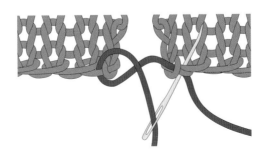

STARTING A NEW PIECE OF YARN WITH SEAMING IN PROGRESS

EVENTUALLY THE yarn you are using to sew a seam will run out and you will have to start a new strand. It is best not to use too long a piece of yarn; 18 to 24 inches is long enough. The friction of pulling longer pieces of yarn through the stitches will wear the yarn thin or pull loosely spun yarns apart.

Turn the work to the wrong side. It isn't necessary to weave in the ends until the seam is complete. Bring the needle with the new yarn up through the same stitch in which you finished the last yarn. Turn to the right side and resume seam as before. There should be no interruption in the flow of the seam. When the seam is completed, turn to the wrong side. Weave the end you dropped upward, and the new tail downward, so the tails cross each other (see "Weaving In Ends," page 130).

First half of seam was worked with green yarn, second half with white yarn. The green tail (yarn dropped) was woven upward and the white tail (new yarn) woven downward. (Different colors of yarn used for illustration purposes only.)

WOVEN SEAMS

THIS TECHNIQUE is the most commonly used method of sewing seams and will yield the most satisfactory results when you are putting a garment together. It is referred to as sewing, but it is really a zigzag or woven-looking stitch. It is also called "weaving a seam." When patterns instruct you to "sew seams," use this technique or one of its variations. To my mind, this is by far the best seam to use for everything except shoulders. For perfect seams, count rows when knitting so matching pieces have the same number of rows. Woven seams will work with any stitch pattern. When using a selvage stitch, sew to the inside of it on both edges.

Benefits
- A version of this seam will work everywhere on a garment.
- Easily worked from the right side of the garment so you can see exactly where you are sewing.
- Makes virtually invisible seams.
- Works well with all weights of yarn.
- Works well with all stitch patterns.
- On pieces that do not have the same number of rows, it's easy to "cheat" to make them fit.
- Can be worked a half stitch or a whole stitch in from the edge.
- Can be worked on every row or every other row.

Drawbacks
- Difficult to find the correct yarn strand in the garment to stitch under.
- Difficult to insert sleeves into armholes because stitch and row gauge are not the same.
- Must work tension consistently.

To Work

Lay pieces flat on a table with right sides facing up, edges to be sewn aligned. Use knitter's safety pins (see "Resources" on page 143) to pin top, middle, and bottom.

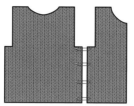

Rows to rows: Using a tail remaining from the cast on, or with a new piece of yarn (see page 62), use your fingers to separate the first and second row of stitches. I prefer to work the seams one stitch in, because it is easier to see where to stitch. *Insert the needle under the horizontal bar between the first and second stitch on the left piece, repeat with the matching row on the right piece.* Repeat from * to * until seam is completed. Go under the cast-off stitch on both sides and weave in the end. If you find that the rows

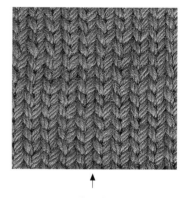

Completed seam

are not matching and one piece is longer than the other piece, you can work under two of the horizontal yarn strands on the side that is too long. Don't do this too often or too close as it will pucker the knitting.

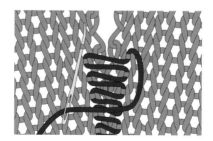

Weaving Side Seam

Stitches to rows: Use this technique when sewing a sleeve into an armhole, especially with drop-shoulder or modified drop-shoulder armholes. *Pin the pieces together. Cut a piece of yarn long enough to weave in the whole sleeve.

Thread a yarn needle with it. Starting at the shoulder seam, bring the needle up from the wrong side on the body side one stitch in from the edge. Pull only half the yarn through. Use the other half of the yarn to work the opposite side of the sleeve seam later.*

Sleeve on Right Sewn to Sweater Body at Left

There is about a three-to-four ratio between stitch and row gauges. The armhole has more rows than the sleeve has stitches. To accommodate this you will need to (work under a whole stitch of the sleeve, but work under only one of the horizontal bars between the first and second stitch on the body side) three times. On the fourth stitch, work under two of the horizontal bars on the armhole side to one whole stitch on the sleeve side. This will take care of the difference in ratio between stitches and rows. Continue in this manner until the sleeve seam is completed. Adjust the ratio of horizontal bars to stitches, if necessary. Go back to the shoulder seam and, using the other end of the yarn, work the other side of the sleeve seam. This should fit the sleeve into the armhole without puckering, provided the sleeve was the correct width to fit the armhole.

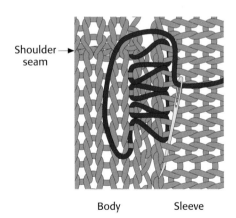

Shoulder seam →

Body   Sleeve

Set in sleeves: Follow from * to * as for stitches to rows on facing page. Work stitches to rows at the top of the sleeve, and work rows to rows for a short time to the area where the bound-off stitches are located at the underarm. Then work stitches to stitches. Accurate pinning is the key to making the sleeve fit into the armhole smoothly. The sleeve cap will look small in comparison with the actual armhole. The bound-off stitches at the top of the sleeve should sit with the center directly at the shoulder seam. Work the seam one stitch in from the edge. There are generally more decreases on the sleeve than on the body of the garment, but when there are matching decreases on both pieces they should line up directly across from each other.

Set-In Sleeve Fit into Armhole

Seams in ribbing: When using traditional cast-on methods where you can choose whether the total number of stitches is an even or an odd number, cast on an even number of stitches if the rib pattern is knit one, purl one. On the

Seam in knit one, purl one ribbing   Seam in knit two, purl two ribbing

wrong side, (purl one, knit one) to the last two stitches, purl two. On the right side, knit two, (purl one, knit one) to the end. This will give a one-stitch seam allowance at both ends of the ribbing. Weave the seam one stitch in at both ends for a perfect seam and no interruption in the rib pattern.

If you are casting on using one of the cast-on methods that yield an odd number of stitches, weave the seam using half of the knit stitch at each edge. When the edges are pulled together there will be one knit stitch, and no interruption in the rib pattern.

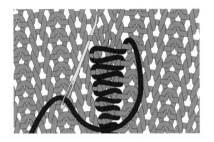

Knit One, Purl One Rib Seam
Woven One Stitch In from Edge

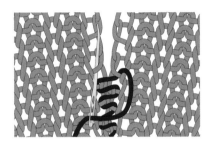

Knit One, Purl One Rib Seam
Woven Half a Stitch In from Edge

For knit two, purl two ribbing, cast on a multiple of four stitches plus two extra. The extra two stitches will be used as selvage stitches. On the wrong side, knit one, (knit two, purl two) to the last stitch, knit one. On the right side, purl one, (knit two, purl two) to the last stitch, purl one. Weave the seam one stitch in at both ends for a perfect seam and no interruption in the rib pattern.

Seams in pattern: When there is a pattern stitch in the knitting, it is best to use a selvage stitch in the body of the garment to make seaming easier. You will have to add the extra stitches to the total number of stitches you are told to cast on. Be sure to work those extra stitches into the armhole shaping, etc., and remember that your stitch count is different from the original directions you may be following. The seams can then be worked as directed above, using a whole stitch, without ruining the flow of the pattern.

Seam in pattern using selvage stitch

Garter Stitch Seams

Garter stitch is a very popular stitch for borders and edges because it lies flat, has great elasticity, and never seems to wear out. Since the seam is virtually invisible on both sides of the work, it is good for sewing together afghan squares or strips of knitting with borders of garter stitch.

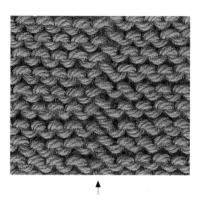

Garter stitch seam

Benefits

- Creates invisible seam.
- Makes joining garter-stitch edges row to row very easy.
- Can be combined with woven seam technique if one edge is garter stitch and the other edge is stockinette stitch.
- Leaves virtually no seam allowance.
- Works well with all weights of yarn.
- Makes counting rows easy—one ridge equals two rows.

Drawbacks

- Pulling too tightly can cause the edge to pucker.
- Need to keep seam as stretchy as the rest of the knitting.
- Sewing too far into the knitting will create a seam allowance; sew just far enough into the edge to draw the two edges together.

To Work

With the two pieces you are joining flat and right side up, pin the pieces together using knitter's safety pins. Start at the lower edge of the right-hand piece, working with new yarn or an existing tail. If the yarn is at the right edge, work into the bottom loop of the "knot" on the left edge and then into the top loop of the knot on the right edge. If the yarn is at the left edge, work into the top loop on the right edge and then into the bottom loop on the left edge.

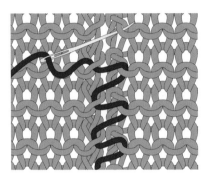

WOVEN SHOULDER SEAMS

This seam is invisible when worked correctly. It is similar to grafting or Kitchener stitch, but is worked with bound-off stitches instead of live stitches. If the yarn used to work the seam is not pulled too tight, the stitches left on top of the bound-off stitches will look like a row of knitting, and the seam allowance will be less bulky. Pulling the yarn tightly will make the new stitches completely disappear, but will leave a thicker seam allowance on the inside.

Right Half, Seaming Yarn Pulled Tightly; Left Half Seaming Yarn (White) Left on Top
(Contrasting yarn used for illustration purposes only.)

Benefits
♦ Makes a seam firm enough to support the weight of the sleeves and neck of a garment.
♦ Works well with all weights of yarn.

Drawbacks
♦ Makes a bulky seam if pulled too tight.
♦ Both bound-off pieces must have the same number of stitches.
♦ Requires that tension must be the same as for the knitting.
♦ Requires consistent tension for the entire seam.

To Work

With the pieces you are joining flat and right side up, pin the pieces together matching the stitches (see page 64). Thread yarn needle with the yarn used to knit the garment. The length of yarn should be long enough to go across the whole shoulder, approximately three times the length of the seam plus 10"–12" extra for tails; adding yarn in the middle can weaken the seam. Insert the yarn needle from back to front, one stitch in from the edge of the front piece; leave a tail long enough to weave in later. Repeat for the back piece. The yarn should stay on top and not loop over the side of the knitting. *Insert the yarn needle under the next whole knit stitch (two strands shaped in a V) on the front piece, keeping the tension so it looks like the rest of the knitting. Repeat from * on the back piece. The two strands shaped in a V will appear upside down on the back piece. Continue working from front piece to back piece from * until all stitches are used. You must use every stitch on both edges. If you choose to tighten the seam yarn so that the stitches are invisible, take both tails and gently pull on them, forcing the new row of knitting to tighten and disappear.

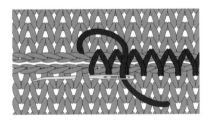

Short-Row Shaping in Preparation for Three-Needle Bind Off

When I use short-row shaping for creating the slope of the shoulders instead of working a stair-step bind off, which is difficult to weave together, I prefer to use three-needle bind off for finishing the seam. The seam is smoother and more even looking than a sewn seam.

There are two versions of short rows. Hold your knitting up to your body as it will be worn. Knit-side short rows are used for the *right* front shoulder and the *left* back shoulder. Purl-side short rows are used for the *left* front shoulder and the *right* back shoulder.

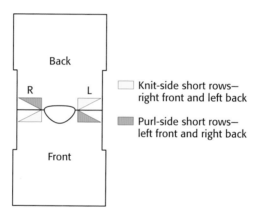

When directions tell you to bind off in sections, you have to start the bind off at the shoulder edge at the beginning of the row. In short-row shaping it will feel like you are doing the opposite of what the directions tell you. You will be working to the stitches that should have been bound off and "leaving" them behind, so to speak, and working a step called wrap and turn (W and T). A small gap will form where you turn in the middle of the row, and you'll have a gap between the stitches on the needle, but you will close the gaps when you work one last row after the short rows are completed. This is called "knitting or purling up the wraps." Trust me; it really is easy. Here is how it works.

Knit-Side Short Rows
(for Right Front Shoulder and Left Back Shoulder)

Knit across the row until the number of stitches you were to bind off remains on the left needle. Work wrap and turn as follows: Slip the next stitch on the left needle to the right needle as if to purl. Move the yarn through the stitches and toward you. Slip the stitch back to the left needle, move the yarn to the back, turn and purl back across the stitches you had previously knit. Work as many short rows as necessary to equal the number of "stair-step" sections that were to be bound off. Knit one final row to pick up the wraps: knit to the first stitch that has the little purl-looking bar where the yarn was wrapped around it. Insert the right knitting needle under the bar or "wrap" on the right side of the work and knit the two stitches together. Continue across, retrieving all wraps as you knit past them. You cannot retrieve the wraps once this final row has been completed. You must knit them as you pass them. Place all stitches on holder. You are now ready to proceed with three-needle bind off.

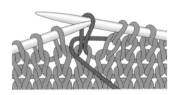

Slip stitch as if to purl. Move yarn to front of work and slip stitch back to left needle.

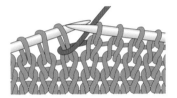

Move yarn to back of work. Turn.

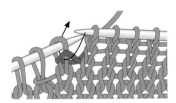

On the final row, knit bar (wrap) and stitch together.

Purl-Side Short Rows
(for Left Front Shoulder and Right Back Shoulder)

Purl across the row until the number of stitches you were to bind off remains on the left needle. Work wrap and turn as follows: Slip the next stitch on the left needle to the right needle as if to purl. Move the yarn through the stitches and away from you. Slip the stitch back to the left needle, move the yarn to the front, turn and knit back across the stitches you had previously purled. Work as many short rows as necessary to equal the number of "stair-step" sections that were to be bound off. Purl one final row to pick up the wraps: purl to the first stitch that has the little purl-looking bar where the yarn was wrapped around it. It will only show on the knit side. Insert the right knitting needle under the bar or "wrap" on the right side of the work and purl the two stitches together. This is a little awkward; be sure the stitch and the loop of the wrap both come off the needle. Continue across, retrieving all wraps as you purl past them. You cannot retrieve the wraps once this final row has been completed. You must purl them as you pass them. Place all stitches on holder. You are now ready to proceed with the three-needle bind off.

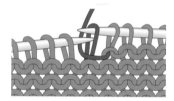

Slip stitch as if to purl. Move yarn
to back of work and slip stitch
back to left needle.

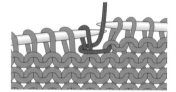

Move yarn toward you. Turn.

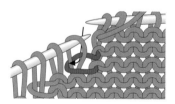

On final row, purl bar (wrap)
and stitch together.

THREE-NEEDLE BIND OFF
FOR SHOULDERS

THE MOST useful place to use this technique is for shoulder seams. When you combine the three-needle bind off with short rows to slope the shoulders of a garment, the result is a perfect seam. (Three-needle bind off can be used on any shoulder bind off, not just those with short-row shaping.) The seam should not be bound off too tightly or it will not lie flat. To prevent this, use a needle in the right hand that is one or two sizes larger than the needle in the left hand. The finished seam is quite flat, yet there is enough area to attach a shoulder pad if desired.

Short-Rowed Shoulders with Three-Needle Bind Off. Wide end is neck edge.

Benefits

♦ Binds off and joins the seam at the same time.

♦ Makes perfect shoulder seams when combined with short rows to make sloped shoulders.

♦ Creates a stable shoulder seam.

♦ Creates a decorative bind off if used on the outside of the garment.

♦ Works with all weights of yarn.

Drawbacks

♦ Requires three needles.

♦ Both seam edges must have the same number of stitches.

♦ Difficult to rip out if a stitch is dropped or worked incorrectly.

♦ Requires more time.

♦ Must be done loosely.

♦ Feels awkward because of the three needles.

To Work

Place stitches to be joined on needles; double-pointed or circular needles work well for this step. The needle points should be at the right with the right sides of the fabric facing. *Knit together one stitch from the front needle and one stitch from the back needle*. Repeat from * to *, adding another stitch to the right needle. When there are two stitches on the right needle, bind off loosely. Continue in this manner until all stitches are knit together and bound off. Cut yarn, finish off.

Knit together one stitch
from front needle and one
stitch from back needle.

Bind off.

KITCHENER STITCH SEAMS

THIS TECHNIQUE is used to weave stitches to stitches and does not really form a seam at all, but a row of knitting placed between the stitches of two pieces. It is used predominantly for toes of socks to prevent bulk where it could rub and cause a blister. If used in the shoulder seam, it creates a slightly weaker seam than the other seam alternatives, but it is delicate and lightweight and works well on delicate fibers or sleeveless items. It is best to use this technique when there isn't much pattern in the knitting as it is difficult to see where to stitch to duplicate the pattern. Maintain tension to match the knitting in the garment.

Benefits
- Good alternative to three-needle bind off.
- Good for toes of socks.
- Creates an invisible seam.
- Works well with all yarns except novelty yarns; stitches may be hard to see and novelty yarn can be difficult to pull through stitch.

Drawbacks
- Takes extra time.
- Must be worked in the same yarn as the garment or yarn will show.
- Requires patience and skill.
- Requires practice before you apply it to garment.
- Easy to lose place; sit in a quiet room with no distractions.
- Best to finish all in one sitting as it can be difficult to determine where you left off.

To Work

Both pieces need to have the same number of stitches. Cut the working yarn about three times the width of the knitting plus about 12" extra to weave in. Thread yarn through a yarn needle. You will direct the yarn needle as if it were a knitting needle. Work with the two pieces on knitting needles with wrong sides together, held in the left hand. Graft the stitches together as follows.

Traditional method: See steps 1–6 on page 55 for directions.
This method will work with stockinette stitch and garter stitch. When worked with garter stitch you must end with a wrong-side row on both pieces.

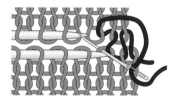

Alternative method:
This method adds some extra steps to the traditional method, but it seems to make the traditional method a bit easier because the work is off the needles. After the knitting has been completed, work four rows of stockinette stitch in a contrasting color cotton yarn. Bind off. Repeat for second piece. Gently press and steam only the contrasting stitches so they are flat and very stable. Do not steam the rest of the knitting. The purpose of the waste yarn is to show you the path to follow to connect the stitches.

Remove waste yarn after seam is completed.

- Fold the waste yarn out of the way and under the knitting. Hold the two pieces to be grafted with right sides facing up, flat on a table.

- Insert the yarn needle from back to front through the first single loop of the knitting on the front piece. Repeat for the back piece. Be sure the yarn stays on top and doesn't loop around the edge of the knitting.

- *Insert the yarn needle under one whole knit stitch (two strands shaped in a V) on the front piece, keeping the tension so it looks like the rest of the knitting. Repeat from the * on the back piece (the two strands shaped in a V will be upside down).

- Continue in this manner until all stitches are used. The tension of the seam should match that of the knitting. You'll notice that your stitches are following the path of the waste yarn.

NOTE: *If your stitches are not following the path of the waste yarn, remove the stitching and start over. Do not remove the knitted waste yarn until you are sure the stitches are in the correct spot. If you skip a stitch or miss one strand of a stitch, the two pieces will not be "knit" together, and the seam will fall apart when the waste knitting is removed.*

GRAFTING LIVE STITCHES TO CAST-ON OR BOUND-OFF STITCHES

THIS TECHNIQUE is included in the grafting or Kitchener stitch section because there are times when one edge will be cast on or bound off and the other edge will have live stitches. This is the technique you would use to graft the cast-on edge of an I-cord to the live stitches at the end of the I-cord. It could also be used to apply a patch pocket that was started with a provisional cast on (see page 24).

Bottom Section: Live Stitches
Top Section: Cast-On or Bound-Off Stitches
(Contrasting yarn used for illustration purposes only.)

To Work

Place the pieces, with right sides up, so that the stitches on the knitting needle are at the bottom and the cast-on or bound-off stitches are at the top. Thread a yarn needle with a tail of the yarn coming from the live stitches. Insert the needle from underneath and upward through the first piece of yarn of the first stitch above the bind off or cast on (the two yarn strands shaped like a V). Then insert the needle into the first live stitch on the knitting needle as if to purl and leave it on the needle. *Insert the needle under the next whole stitch on the finished edge, then into the first live stitch on the knitting needle as if to knit. Drop the stitch from the needle. Insert the yarn needle into the next stitch on the knitting needle as if to purl. Leave the stitch on the needle. Repeat from * to * until all stitches are gone from the knitting needle and the bound-off edge. Finish off.

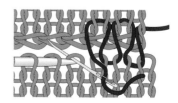

PATCH POCKET SEAMS

POCKETS ARE a great addition to most sweaters, but if attached poorly they will destroy the perfect finishing you may have already accomplished. Patch pockets can be any size, but the average size for cardigans should be about 5" to 6" wide by 6" to 7" long. For most sweaters, the bottom of the pocket should be placed about 20" to 22" from the shoulder, longer for tall men or women, and about 2" to 3" from the center front.

TIP: *If you work pockets in garter stitch or seed stitch it will be easier to hide the pocket seams. Be sure to leave a one-stitch seam allowance at each end of the pocket border.*

White Patch Pocket Sewn to Purple Background

Benefits

+ Pockets can be attached as decorative element on surface of knitting.
+ Pockets that weren't planned from the beginning of work can be attached.
+ Works with all weights of yarn.

Drawbacks

+ Difficult to achieve a smooth seam line.
+ Must be done in line with the rows of knitting. Once a row is chosen it must be used consistently.
+ Will destroy a garment if pocket is attached incorrectly.
+ Requires skill and patience.

To Work

Block the pocket and the piece to which it will be applied. Pin the pocket in place with knitter's safety pins. Using another color yarn, preferably cotton, baste the pocket in place and then baste around the pocket to help you sew the seam straight; baste one stitch away from the edge of the pocket. Starting at an upper corner of the pocket, weave the side of the pocket to the garment as you would a side seam (see page 64), using half of a stitch on the pocket and the running thread between two stitches on the garment. Weave the bottom of the pocket as you would a shoulder seam, stitch to stitch. Weave the other side of the pocket as you worked the first side. Secure firmly.

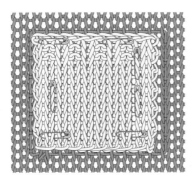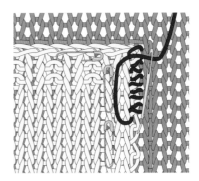

An alternative method for starting the pocket would be to use a provisional cast on (see page 24) to knit the pocket, remove the cast on, and place the stitches on a knitting needle. Weave the pocket as described above, but when you get to the stitches on the knitting needle, weave the bottom seam as though you were grafting live stitches to bound-off stitches (see page 80).

INSET POCKET SEAMS

INSET POCKETS require a pocket lining and an opening in the garment for the pocket. This opening must be made as the garment is being knit. The pocket lining is then sewn on the inside of the garment, instead of on the outside like the patch pocket. Again, the challenge is to sew the pocket to the garment without distorting the knitting. The sewing is all on the inside, so you must be careful that the stitches do not show through on the right side.

Ribbing for Top of Pocket Opening on Right Side

White Pocket Lining Sewn to Wrong Side

Benefits

♦ More invisible than the patch pocket.

♦ Works well with all weights of yarn.

Drawbacks

♦ Can be difficult to sew pocket without showing on the right side.

♦ Pocket opening must be planned before knitting piece where pocket will be placed.

♦ Border must be knit to the top of the opening after the garment is completed.

♦ Requires a lot of steaming to lie flat, but steaming must be done carefully so it does not flatten work.

♦ Can be difficult to match the seam for the pocket border and the seam on the inside to attach the pocket.

To Work

Knit the pocket lining to the desired dimensions and place the stitches on a holder; set aside. Work garment to area where top of pocket is to be placed. Knit to the pocket opening, place the same number of stitches on a holder as were used for the pocket lining, place the pocket-lining stitches on the left needle, knit across the pocket stitches and finish the row. Sew the pocket lining down later.

An alternative method I use to make the pocket fit the opening better is to make the pocket lining two stitches wider than desired. Place the stitches on a holder and set aside. Knit to one stitch before the pocket opening. Slip the next stitch to the right needle. Place the same number of stitches that were used for the pocket lining minus two from the garment on a holder. Place the pocket-lining stitches on the left needle. Slip stitch on right needle back to left needle. Work SSK with the next two stitches—one from the garment and one from the pocket lining. Knit to one stitch from the end of the pocket lining and knit two together—last stitch from the pocket lining and next stitch from the garment. Finish row.

By working the extra steps of knitting stitches together at the beginning and end of the pocket, you create less of a hole when the pocket is sewn to the wrong side of the garment. It is then easier to add the ribbing or border at the top of the pocket, and sewing it to the front is easier and less obvious.

To attach the pocket made with either method above to the inside of the work: Block the pocket and the piece to which it will be sewn. Pin the pocket in place. Using another color yarn, baste around the pocket to help you sew the seam straight, basting one stitch away from the edge of the pocket. On the wrong side of the garment, weave the edge stitch of the pocket to a purl bar or the running thread between two stitches as you work down the side. At the bottom, whipstitch from a purl bar to the cast on of the pocket. Complete the other side as you worked the first side.

An alternative method for starting the pocket would be to use a provisional cast on (see page 24), remove the cast on, and overcast each stitch to a purl bar across the bottom.

Pocket border: For both inset-pocket methods, place the stitches on the holder on the appropriate-sized knitting needle and work the desired border. Be sure to leave a one-stitch seam allowance at each end. Weave the edges of the border to the front of the garment, in line with the seam of the pocket worked on the inside.

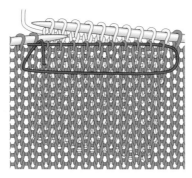

Front of Garment Placed on Stitch Holder
Knit across pocket.

PICKING UP STITCHES

ENERALLY, PICKING up stitches for neckbands, armholes, or any edge is the last step in finishing a garment. If it is done poorly, it will show terribly. In general, the knitting of the bands is done in another direction than the knitting of the garment and it is in a new stitch pattern, so the eye will go to any errors made. Neckbands, since they are located right under your face, are generally the first thing on your sweater a person might look at, and you want them to be perfect in fit and appearance.

The most popular and successful way to pick up stitches is to knit the new stitches onto a knitting needle. This technique is simple to learn and leaves the best results. It feels just like normal knitting, but with a knitting needle in the right hand and the garment in the left hand. Even if you are a continental knitter, you will find this technique the easiest to use.

Don't try to pick up stitches with the yarn in your left hand; in your left hand you can't hold the yarn in the correct position to bring the new stitch through. Holding it in the right hand allows you to pull back on the yarn, helping the new stitch "pop" through the knitting.

The general rule is to pick up stitches with the right side of the work facing. There are a few exceptions: in some collars, for instance. But if the pattern doesn't tell you, always pick up stitches from the right side of the work.

Occasionally you may find loose areas in the knitting where you need to pick up stitches. When this happens, insert the knitting needle into the knitting, pick up the purl bar of the stitch or row next to it, and knit the two stitches together.

If you find after picking up stitches that a stitch or two is loose or a hole is forming in the next row, knit or purl into the back of the stitch to help tighten it up. You can only do this on the first row after picking up the stitches.

In general, the formula for picking up stitches is to pick up every stitch or row on cast-off edges or edges that have shaping, and pick up three out of every four stitches on straight edges, or against edges with rows. This accommodates the different stitch and row gauge as well as makes the curves lie flat.

When a pattern tells you how many stitches to pick up, use the above formula. But it is also helpful to divide the edge into smaller sections. Using knitter's safety pins, fold a section in half and mark, fold in quarters and mark, and so on. This will help you pick up the same number of stitches in each section. It will also minimize the number of stitches you have to rip out if you don't have the correct number of stitches at the end. You'll only have to rip out a section if you don't have the correct number of stitches in it, and that's easier than ripping out the entire edge and starting over.

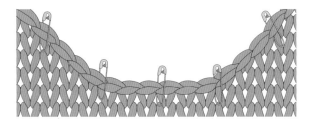

There are cases where you would pick up stitches using a combination of all of the following techniques. An armhole on a vest is the best example. First, use safety pins to mark off the straight edge of the armhole above the decreases into three or four sections. Starting at the side seam, pick up every stitch across the bound-off stitches at the base of the armhole and every stitch on the curved edge where the decreases are. Then pick up three stitches out of four rows from the straight edge of the armhole to the shoulder seam. Repeat in reverse for the other armhole. Be sure to pick up the same number of stitches in each section. That is, the bound-off areas should have the same number, the edges with decreases should have the same number, and the straight edges should have the same number.

TO WORK

WITH CIRCULAR needles for large areas, or a straight needle for small areas, *insert the needle into the knitting, wrap the yarn around the needle, and bring the new stitch through. Repeat from * until you have picked up the desired number of stitches. It will feel like you are pulling the knitting in the left hand over the new stitch, not like the new stitch is coming through the knitting as it would normally come through a stitch on the left needle.

PICKING UP STITCHES ON A BOUND-OFF EDGE

EXAMPLE: *Front or back neck bound-off stitches.*

INSERT THE knitting needle into the center of the first stitch, which looks like a V. Pick up the stitch as directed above. Continue across the edge, picking up one stitch into each bound-off stitch across. There will be the two strands of yarn of the V between each picked-up stitch.

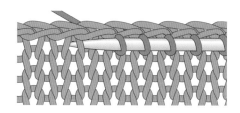

PICKING UP STITCHES ON AN EDGE WITH ROWS OF KNITTING

EXAMPLES: *Part of a neck or sleeve opening, or the front band of a cardigan.*

INSERT THE knitting needle between two purl bars, one stitch in from the edge. Pick up stitches across the edge, inserting the knitting needle between the purl bars for the entire edge. Use the ratio of picking up three stitches out of every four rows. Once you have chosen the row in which you are picking up stitches, do not change. Remain in that row for the entire edge.

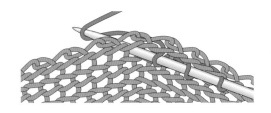

PICKING UP STITCHES ON AN EDGE WITH DECREASES

EXAMPLES: *V necks, or armhole edges.*

WHEN YOU have worked decreases with a one-stitch seam allowance, insert the needle under a whole stitch for the seam allowance between the purl bars and pick up the new stitch. Remember to pick up all stitches leaving the one-stitch selvage. If you don't pick up whole stitches on the edge, they will not appear neat and holes will form on the body of the sweater because the weight and pull of the band will stretch out the stitches.

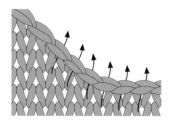

Stitches Picked Up on Curved
Edge with Decreases

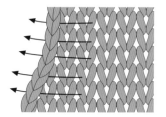

Stitches Picked Up on
V Neck with Decreases

Stitches Picked Up for Round Neck

Stitches Picked Up for V Neck

Stitches Picked Up for Armhole

BORDERS, BANDS, AND FINISHES

*A*LMOST EVERYTHING knitted needs some kind of a border or band to create a finished look and to make the edges lie flat. You can attach these later or knit them simultaneously with the piece. There are several methods you can use to work a border or band; many of them are utilitarian and some of them are just plain fun. Each one has its place; it all depends on what you're knitting and what you want the finished piece to look like. An example of this is when a garter-stitch band is knit at the same time as the front of a stockinette-stitch cardigan. Because garter stitch has more rows per inch than stockinette, it will be shorter than the stockinette section. It can be blocked to match in most cases, but not always. The purpose of the front bands is also to keep the edges from rolling. Often when garter stitch is used for the border with a stockinette body, it has to be very wide to keep the edge flat. The best methods for applying bands are to pick up stitches and work the band out from the garment, or to knit a band separately and sew it on.

Some borders can be knit along with the body of the knitting. But this method doesn't work for all edges. A border can end up being too short for the length of the garment, which will pull up the garment edge.

These finishes are what will make your knit garment beautiful. Unfortunately, if they are done poorly, they can ruin the garment. Your knitting skills will really shine when you take the time to learn and work these correctly.

HEMS

A HEM can help a garment drape nicely, especially in a long coat in a medium to worsted-weight yarn. However, a hem can also add bulk to the bottom edge. To keep the added thickness to a minimum, work the area that turns under on a needle at least two sizes smaller.

To work the hem and make it more invisible, knit the cast-on stitches together with the hem stitches (see page 93). To seam a hem and the side seam, seam the hem first and then the side seam.

Hem with Stockinette Fold Line

Hem with Purl Fold Line

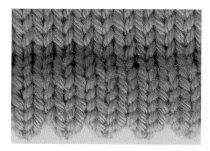

Hem with Picot Fold Line

Benefits

♦ Firm border replaces ribbing or any border stitch.

♦ Works well on a garment that does not need to be fitted at bottom edge.

♦ Works on garment lower edges as well as on bands at neck and front.

♦ Works with any stitch pattern, but stockinette stitch is the preferred pattern.

♦ Works well with most weights of yarns.

Drawbacks

- ♦ Can be thick, requires a lot of steaming to lie flat.
- ♦ Takes more than usual amount of time.
- ♦ Takes more yarn than a rib or garter-stitch border would.
- ♦ Must be worked on smaller needle to start.
- ♦ Can pull up the length of the garment; be sure to measure accurately.
- ♦ Will not lie flat if hem is less than ½" wide; will roll to the knit side.

To Work

Stockinette fold line: Using the provisional cast on (page 24) and needles two sizes smaller than called for, cast on the number of stitches required. Work the required length for the hem, ending with a purl row. Change to specified larger needle size and work the same number of rows in stockinette stitch. Remove the provisional cast on and place the stitches on the smaller knitting needle. Fold the hem so that the two needles are parallel to each other, the hem needle in back with wrong sides together. With a third needle, knit one stitch from the front needle and one stitch from the back needle together across the row. You will be one stitch short on the hem needle; work the last body stitch by itself. Continue in pattern on larger needle.

Knit stitches from the front
and back needles together.

Purl fold line: Work as above, but when changing back to the original needle, work a purl row on the right side of the work. Finish as above.

Picot fold line: Work as above, but when changing back to the original needle, work as follows on right side for even number of stitches: Knit one, (yarn over, knit two together) across, end with knit one. Or for odd number of stitches: (Knit two together, yarn over) across, end knit one. Finish as above.

FOLDED OR HEMMED NECKBANDS

USING THIS technique will result in a neckband that is easy to pull over the head. It also leaves a more professional looking finish. Working in the round on circular needles means no seam, which will make the band smoother. This technique mirrors a hemmed border at the bottom of the garment.

Right Side of Hemmed Neckband

On wrong side, note that band covers edge where stitches were picked up.

Benefits

♦ Good for crew necks; results in a neckband easy to pull over head.
♦ Good for children's and baby sweaters.
♦ Leaves smooth finish at the neck.
♦ Places more knitting at the neck edge, where there is greater wear.
♦ Works well with all weights of yarn.
♦ Used with circular or flat bands.
♦ Can be worked in stockinette or ribbing.

Drawbacks

♦ Takes more than usual amount of time.
♦ Neckband is heavier and thicker than a typical single-layer ribbed or garter-stitch neckband.
♦ When sewing the band down it is easy to skip a stitch and make the band twist at an angle.
♦ Double band of ribbing will add thickness; work inside layer in stockinette stitch on a smaller needle instead of ribbing to decrease bulk.

To Work

Pick up the required number of stitches around the neck. If you are working in the round, be sure to pick up the correct multiple of stitches for the pattern you have chosen. For example, pick up an even number of stitches for knit one, purl one, or a multiple of four stitches for knit two, purl two. If working with a seam, leave a selvage stitch at each end. Work the ribbing or pattern stitch as directed. When band is wide enough, change to smaller needles and work a fold line of your choice, or one that matches the hem at bottom edge of the knitting (see page 92). Continue pattern stitch for same number of rows as for the front of the band. Do not bind off. Cut yarn approximately three times the diameter of the neck opening, and whipstitch each stitch down loosely, covering the selvage remaining from picking up the stitches; finish off. Pull out on the neckband as you work the whipstitching to be sure it is stretchy and you are not sewing too tightly.

Whipstitch neckband to inside of neck edge.

NOTE: *This technique can be used for front bands of cardigans too, but it is quite thick for button bands and buttonhole bands. Buttonholes would need to be placed in both bands and sewn together with buttonhole stitch.*

KNITTED-ON BUTTON BANDS

THIS IS one of the most commonly used button bands. Ribbing is the most common stitch used, but garter stitch and seed stitch will work as well. For a more elastic edge, use knit two, purl two ribbing instead of knit one, purl one.

The biggest problems with knitted-on button bands come from picking up too many or too few stitches. Too many stitches will result in a band that is too long for the body or edge of the garment. Too few stitches and the band will be too short and pull up from the bottom and down from the top, and will not hang properly. In general, when working the band in ribbing, you should pick up three stitches for every four rows of knitting to get the correct ratio of stitches in the band and rows in the body. This formula will work for all weights of yarn except bulky yarn; with bulky yarn it may be necessary to pick up stitches on every row because the row and stitch gauges are more similar.

Benefits
+ Tends to be easier than other methods for most knitters.
+ Easy to work buttonholes into the band.
+ Used to control the curve on the edge of a piece of knitting.
+ Works well with all weights of yarn.

Drawbacks
+ Easy to pick up too many or too few stitches.
+ Uses one row of knitting for picked-up stitches; may require a selvage stitch for a complete pattern stitch to be left on the body.
+ For a folded buttonhole band, you must work buttonholes on both outer and inner layers before sewing band together. Sew buttonholes together with buttonhole stitch.

To Work

Using sweater yarn and needle used for bottom border, pick up appropriate number of stitches on edge (see page 86) using a one-stitch seam allowance. Pick up every stitch in the ribbing or border at the bottom edge to prevent the bottom edge from pulling up at the front. Work ribbing or stitch pattern for the band; bind off loosely. A hemmed band could be worked here as well (see page 92).

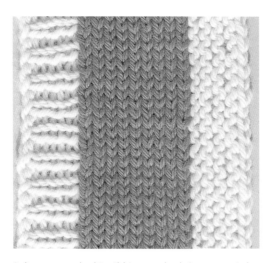

Picked up stitches are worked in ribbing on the left, garter stitch on the right.

TIP: *For garter stitch bands, bind off on wrong side, creating the last ridge and leaving the stitches remaining from binding off on the wrong side.*

SEWN-ON BUTTON BANDS

THIS IS a wonderful technique for any cardigan, but you must plan ahead because you need to start the band when the ribbing for the bottom band is worked. Attaching the band requires careful sewing so that the seam is absolutely invisible. Add an extra stitch for a seam allowance on the border to make it easier to sew to the garment.

Button Band Worked with
Existing Stitches from Ribbing

Button Band to Edge
without Existing Stitches

Benefits

- Creates a very firm border.
- Seam is virtually invisible when used with a seam allowance.
- Works well with all weights of yarn.
- Controls the curve on the edge of a piece of knitting.
- Works with a variety of stitch patterns.

Drawbacks

- Requires precise sewing.
- Must be knit firmly to support edge of garment.
- If made too long, the front edge will hang too long; if made too short, the front edge will be too short and pull up the bottom edge.
- Buttonhole placement is generally calculated after the garment has been completed, but you may need to make a buttonhole while the bottom border is being knit.

To Work

With existing stitches from ribbing: In most cases, instructions for this technique will direct you to cast on enough stitches for the bottom band and the front band. After the ribbing for the bottom band is completed, place the stitches for the front band on a holder and knit the body of the garment as directed. When the body is completed, place the stitches for the front band, which are on the holder, on the smaller ribbing needle. Cast on one stitch using cable cast on at the inside edge, leaving a long tail with which to sew the band to the body later. Continue in ribbing as set, working extra stitch in stockinette stitch. *When it appears that you have most of the ribbing completed for the front band, pin the band to the front edge. Begin weaving the seam together (see page 64), using one stitch of the body and the extra stitch added to the ribbing; it should match row by row.

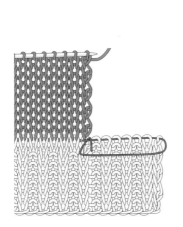

If you counted rows on the body and rows on the border, the seam should match perfectly. You should not have to stretch the band very much; the ribbing is shorter because it was worked on a smaller needle. If you find that the band is not lying straight and flat against the body of the garment, adjust the seam by working under two purl bars instead of one. You can add more to the front-band ribbing if it is too short, or remove rows if it is too long. Bind off*.

Without existing stitches: Cast on the required number of stitches for the front band plus one extra stitch for a seam allowance, worked in stockinette stitch. Work in ribbing or pattern stitch. Proceed from * to * above.

Zippers

Separating zippers are a wonderful alternative to buttons. A heavyweight zipper, such as those used in outerwear clothing, is the perfect addition to a bulky jacket. The front will close without gaps and keep the cold air out.

Zippers are hand sewn to the knitting to prevent stretching the knitted edge out of shape. It is so easy to stretch the knitting when inserting a zipper that care must be taken to be sure the zipper fits the edge, without stretching the knitting.

Plastic separating zippers come in an array of colors and lengths. If you cannot find a zipper the length to fit the opening, buy a longer one and cut it to fit. With a sewing machine, zigzag across the zipper teeth just above where you want the zipper to end. Work very dense stitches for about ½". Cut the extra length of the zipper above the stitching, leaving enough room to hide the stitched area in a seam or on the inside of the knitting.

Benefits

- Great for heavier jackets.
- Good alternative when a garment is too small to overlap in the front for buttons.
- Used as decorative alternative to buttons.

Drawbacks

- Difficult to keep zipper in position while sewing.
- Knitting can stretch while sewing in zipper.
- Sweater is either open or closed; unlike with buttons, you can't close just one area.
- Will make front bands a little stiffer and thicker.

To Work

The knitting should have a firm edge to which you can attach the zipper. Either a two-stitch selvage or a row of single crochet will work well. Pin the zipper in position; be sure the borders match at the bottom when the zipper is closed. Normally, the zipper would be covered with fabric so it doesn't show, but this is difficult with a knitted garment because the knitting tends to catch in the teeth of the zipper. Try to get the edge of the knitting as close as you can to the zipper. Baste the zipper in place with contrasting sewing thread. With a backstitch and matching sewing thread, sew the zipper to the wrong side of the knitting through the center of the fabric at the side of the zipper. Be careful the stitching doesn't show on the right side. On the right side, sew the knitting to the edge of the zipper with small stitches that won't show, also using matching sewing thread. Remove the basting. If one side does not match the other side exactly, re-stitch it.

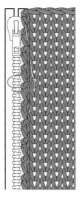
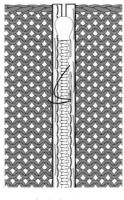
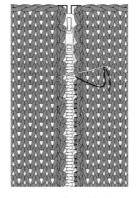

| Baste to front. | Backstitch zipper to wrong side. | Overcast edge of knitting to right side. |

Attached I-Cord

This technique leaves a lovely vertically knit rolled edge that covers a bound-off area. It can be used to finish a collar, pocket, or border. Applied I-cord, a version of this border, can be applied to the edges of the garment for uniformity (see page 56).

If you are working I-cord around an edge where the I-cord will need to be seamed, do not bind off when completed; sew two ends of the I-cord together by grafting the cast-on edge to the live stitches still on the needle (see page 80).

Benefits

- Worked as an edging, after stitches are bound off, or on the edge of knitting.
- Creates a decorative edge.
- Useful for making buttonholes (see page 111) while attaching the I-cord to a front edge.
- Works well with all weights of yarn.
- Generally worked over three stitches, but can be worked on two to five stitches depending on weight of yarn.
- Can be worked on right or wrong side of knitting.

Drawbacks

- Must be worked loosely over a large area, or it will cause the knitting to pucker.
- Easy to pick up too many or too few stitches.
- Takes more yarn than pattern may call for.
- Adds time to finishing process.

Tip: *It is important to work the attached I-cord loosely enough so that you don't pucker the edges of the knitting. To do this, use a needle two sizes larger or more in the right hand, depending on where you are attaching the I-cord. For example, to help a shawl collar stay flat, start out with a smaller needle in the right hand; then switch to a larger needle as you work the back of the collar. The larger needle can be up to three or four sizes larger than the original needle.*

To Work

With picked-up stitches: On the bound-off or cast-on edge, pick up every stitch using a circular needle the size the knitting was worked in. On an edge with rows, pick up three out of four stitches using the same needle as above. With the knitting in the left hand, cast on three stitches using the cable cast on (page 14). *Knit two stitches, pulling the yarn tightly across the back of the three stitches, forming a tube, work SSK with the last stitch of the three stitches just cast on and one stitch from the picked up stitches. Slip the three stitches just knit back to the left needle and repeat from * until all stitches that were picked up are used.

Attached I-Cord Worked with Stitches on Knitting Needle

With no stitches on knitting needle: With two double-pointed needles, same size as used for knitting, cast on three stitches. Do not turn; slide stitches to other end of needle. *Knit two stitches, pulling yarn tightly across the back to make a tube, slip the third stitch, and pick up one stitch into the knitted edge and pass the slipped stitch over. Slip the three stitches just knit back to the left needle and repeat from * until edge is covered with I-cord. Be careful not to pick up stitches too close together or too far apart. (See "Picking Up Stitches", page 86.)

Attached I-Cord Worked with No Stitches on Knitting Needle

Slip Stitch Crochet

You can use slip stitch crochet alone or as the foundation for other crochet stitches. When used alone on the edge of knitting, it will not keep stockinette stitch from rolling. It is a very useful technique for keeping shoulders and neck from sagging with the weight of the sleeves or from loose knitting.

Slip stitch crochet to bound-off edge.

Benefits

- Can be used to join a row of single crochet, including reverse single crochet.
- Can be used to reinforce necks and shoulders of garments.
- Can be used before a row of reverse single crochet.
- Can be used on all edges without adding length to the piece, but has no stretch.
- Can be worked with right side or wrong side facing.

Drawbacks

- Easy to work too tightly. (But should be worked *firmly* when used to stabilize shoulder seams.)
- Can cause edges of knitting to pucker if spacing of stitches is not correct.
- If used as an edging, will not stretch.

To Work

Work from right to left with the right side or wrong side of the knitting facing you. Insert hook into knitting, yarn over hook, pull loop of yarn through. *Insert hook into next stitch of knitting, yarn over hook, pull loop of yarn through the stitch and the loop on the hook.* When using for shoulder or neck reinforcement, use a hook one to two sizes smaller than the knitting needle and work through both layers of seam allowance with firm stitches. Repeat from * to * for width of seam, finish off.

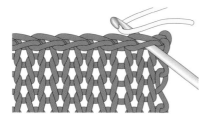

Insert hook into stitch, yarn over hook.

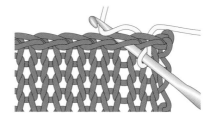

Insert hook into stitch, yarn over hook.

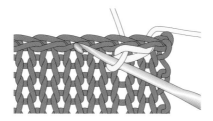

Pull loop of yarn through stitch
and loop on hook.

To join single crochet, insert needle under the chain at the top of stitch to be joined. Pull up a loop of yarn and pull through loop on the hook. Finish off.

TIP: *To compare crochet hook to knitting needle, use a needle gauge. Insert the crochet hook into the hole for the size that is two sizes smaller than the knitting needle used. You can compare the millimeter sizes of the knitting needles and the crochet hooks on the needle gauge.*

SINGLE CROCHET

THIS VERY simple technique can be added to any knitted edge that won't end up in a seam. It requires more than one row to keep a stockinette edge from rolling. Use a crochet hook one or two sizes smaller than the knitting needle used. Check the size with a needle gauge (see page 105).

Use a single crochet border to pull in a too-large border by skipping stitches, but be careful not to reduce the edge so much that it is too short or too small. It should be slightly stretchy to match the knitting.

One Row of Single Crochet

Two Rows of Single Crochet

Benefits

♦ Perfect border option for knitted edges.

♦ Works with all weights of yarn.

♦ Easy to add buttonholes (see page 111).

♦ Can be firm or lacy.

♦ Both decorative and utilitarian.

♦ Provides good base for other crochet edges.

Drawbacks

♦ Can be difficult to work correct ratio of crochet stitches
   to knitted stitches (see "Picking up Stitches," page 86).

♦ Corresponding edges should have same number of stitches.

♦ If extra stitches aren't worked at corners, the corners will roll.

♦ One row of single crochet will not keep stockinette stitch from rolling.

To Work

Work from right to left with the right side of the knitting facing you. Insert
hook into knitting, yarn over hook, pull loop of yarn through the knitting to
the front, yarn over hook and pull it through the first loop. *Insert hook into
next stitch of knitting, yarn over hook, pull loop of yarn through the stitch,
yarn over hook and pull through both loops on hook. Repeat from * to end of
row. Skip or add stitches if necessary to keep the edge flat.

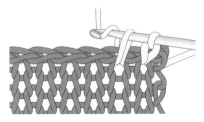

Insert hook into stitch, yarn over hook,
pull loop through to front, yarn over hook.

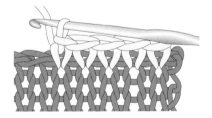

Pull loop through both loops on hook.

To work multiple rows of single crochet, turn the work at the end of the
row, chain one, and work as above, inserting hook under both loops of the V
lying on its side at the top edge of the previous row.

Reverse Single Crochet
or Crab Stitch

This stitch is worked for only one row and is a final edging. It adds a finishing touch to any piece of knitting. No further crochet can be added after this row. To finish off, join first and last stitch with a slip stitch if done in the round, or finish off and weave in ends if done on straight edges. This stitch by itself will not add a lot of width to the border and will not keep stockinette stitch from rolling.

Reverse Single Crochet over Bound-Off Stitches

Benefits

- Used as final finish to a row of crochet or knitting.
- Creates charming border for necks and front edges.
- Simple to work on any knit or crochet edge.
- Works well with all weights of yarn.

Drawbacks

- Can't be worked on an edge that is to be seamed.
- No other rows of crochet or knitting can be added after this stitch is worked.
- Easy to work too tightly, but steam helps to stretch it out slightly.
- If worked in a yarn that is "scratchy" it will feel scratchier due to knot at top of stitch.
- Feels awkward, because it is worked "backward."
- Takes some practice to learn.
- Stockinette stitch with reverse crochet applied will not lie flat; multiple rows of single crochet or a non-rolling border should be worked first.

To Work

If working in the round, work a row (or rows) of single crochet on the edge, join with a slip stitch, do not turn. If working flat, chain one at end of row, do not turn. *Insert hook into first stitch to the right, yarn over hook, pull loop of yarn to front of work, yarn over hook, and pull through both loops on hook*. Repeat from * to * until all stitches are used. The stitch will appear twisted and slightly raised in a little knot. Stitches on hook are in a different order than in single crochet.

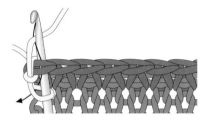

Join yarn with slip stitch.
Insert hook into first stitch
to the right.

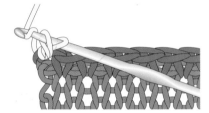

Yarn over hook, pull through
both loops on hook.

To work directly into the knitting, work as above, inserting the crochet hook into the knitting below the cast-on or bound-off edge, starting at the left end with right side facing.

BUTTONHOLES

*T*HESE SMALL but important holes probably cause more problems in knitting than any other feature. The problem is that it is difficult to make them look as neat and tidy as we'd like them to, and they can stretch out of shape easily because of the general nature of knitting. It is best to keep them as small as possible so they do not stretch out from the button going through over and over.

It's important that the buttonhole "fit" into the knitting. This means you should have the button before you start the buttonholes, to make the right size and type of buttonhole. When you make the buttonhole first, you're likely to spend days or weeks searching for the correct button. I've done it myself. Now I carry the gauge swatch in my purse while the garment is being knit so I can search for buttons whenever the opportunity presents itself.

To space your buttonholes evenly requires a little math. Measuring isn't accurate enough; you need to count rows or stitches. To do this, make the front band without the buttonholes first and then use it to count rows or stitches for proper placement of the buttonholes on the opposite front. For women's garments make the left front band first; for men's garments, make the right front band first. See the worksheet on page 140 to calculate the placement.

TWO-ROW BUTTONHOLE (HORIZONTAL)

THIS IS the most commonly used buttonhole. This buttonhole takes two rows to work; that means you must count two rows for every buttonhole when calculating their placement.

The bound-off edge of this buttonhole does not match the cast-on edge very well. You can hide this discrepancy by reinforcing the buttonhole with the buttonhole stitch (see page 126). However, the buttonhole stitch will reduce the size of the buttonhole, so you should start out by making a larger buttonhole.

The traditional two-row buttonhole is one of the most common, but the technique leaves a small hole in the right-hand corner. I developed a revised two-row buttonhole to eliminate the small hole.

Left: Traditional Two-Row Buttonhole
Right: Revised Two-Row Buttonhole
Top to Bottom: Ribbing, Stockinette Stitch, and Garter Stitch

Benefits

♦   Works with any number of stitches.
♦   Works with all weights of yarn.
♦   Works well with any stitch pattern.
♦   Can be worked on right or wrong side of knitting.

Drawbacks

- Results aren't always satisfactory.
- Easily distorts the knitting.
- Can stretch out of shape and become too large for button if not reinforced.
- Top of the bound-off edge of the buttonhole doesn't match the cast-on edge at the bottom, and there is a bit of a hole in the right corner.

To Work

Traditional two-row buttonhole: Work to position of buttonhole. *Work two more stitches and begin bind off for number of stitches needed to make correct size buttonhole. Finish the row. On the next row, work to the bound-off stitches, turn the work, cast on the number of stitches bound off using the knitted-on cast on (see page 12). Turn the work and finish the row.*

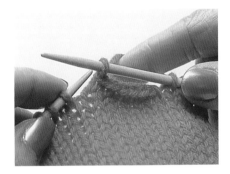

Cast off stitches.

Cast on new stitches.

Revised two-row buttonhole (almost a three-row buttonhole): Work to position of buttonhole from * to * above. On the next row, work into the back of the cast-on stitches and the first stitch after the cast-on stitches; continue knitting.

Knit into back of stitches.

ONE-ROW BUTTONHOLE (HORIZONTAL)

THIS BUTTONHOLE leaves a cleaner, smoother edge at the top and bottom of the buttonhole than the two-row buttonhole. The traditional way of making it can leave a small gap or loose area at the right end. I added a couple of steps to eliminate this problem. I recommend that you make a sample to be sure your button will go through the buttonhole; it is slightly tighter once completed.

This buttonhole takes one row to work; that means you must count one row for every buttonhole when calculating the placement of the buttonholes.

Left: Original One-Row Buttonhole
Right: Revised One-Row Buttonhole
Top to Bottom: Ribbing, Stockinette Stitch, and Garter Stitch

Benefits

- Makes a neater buttonhole than two-row buttonhole.
- Requires no reinforcing.
- Works with all weights of yarn.
- Works with any number of stitches.
- Works well with any stitch pattern.
- Yields tighter buttonhole with firmer edges than two-row buttonhole.
- Can be worked on right or wrong side of knitting.

Drawbacks

- Takes more time than two-row buttonhole.
- Not completely perfect, but still the best option for a larger buttonhole.
- Leaves a loop of yarn over left end of a stitch that looks like a purl bar.
- Can pull the knitting toward the center of buttonhole on both ends.

To Work

Original method: Work to position of buttonhole. Move yarn forward, slip a stitch purlwise, move the yarn to the back. *Slip a stitch purlwise from the left needle to the right needle, pass the second stitch on the right needle over the first stitch, as if to bind off. Repeat from * for as many stitches as needed to accommodate the button. Slip the last bound-off stitch from the right needle back to the left needle. Turn the work. Using the cable cast on (see page 14), **cast on one more stitch than you bound off. Turn the work. Slip the first stitch on the left needle over to the right needle and pass the extra cast-on stitch on the right needle over to close the buttonhole. Continue knitting.

Move yarn forward, slip stitch purlwise.

Pass second stitch over first stitch.

Cast on one extra stitch.

Revised method: Everything remains the same as for original method (facing) to **. Cast on three more stitches than you bound off. Turn the work. Slip the first stitch on the left needle over to the right needle and pass the extra cast-on stitch on the right needle over to close the buttonhole. Finish the row. On the next row, work to one stitch before the cast-on stitches of the buttonhole, purl two together if the stitch is to be a purl, or knit two together if it is to be a knit, work to last stitch of cast-on stitches and work slip, slip, purl if stitch is to be a purl, or slip, slip, knit if stitch is to be a knit. Finish row. The extra step of knitting or purling the stitches together at the beginning and end of the cast-on stitches helps to close up the gaps and clean up the corners of the buttonhole.

Purl two together on return row at beginning of buttonhole.

Slip, slip, purl at end of buttonhole.

YARN-OVER BUTTONHOLE

THIS BUTTONHOLE is almost invisible, and can be used virtually anywhere as long as the chosen button will go through. If worked in knit one, purl one ribbing, the required decrease can be hidden under the knit stitch before or after the yarn over, making the buttonhole even more invisible. See "Small Version" below.

The size of the needle and the weight of the yarn will determine the size of the buttonhole and the button used. This buttonhole takes one row to work; that means you must count one row for every buttonhole when calculating the placement of the buttonholes.

Small Version　　　　Larger Version
Top to Bottom: Ribbing, Stockinette Stitch, and Garter Stitch

Benefits

- Almost invisible.
- Does not require any finishing.
- Works with all weights of yarn.
- Works with any stitch pattern.
- Very simple to work.

Drawbacks

- May not wear well; this buttonhole has no finishing or bound-off stitches.
- Easy to catch buttons with sharp edges or points on the loop at top of buttonhole and possibly tear or fray the yarn.

To Work

Small version: In non-rib stitch, work to position of buttonhole, knit two together, yarn over needle. In ribbing, work to position of buttonhole. If there is a knit then a purl stitch before the yarn over is to be placed, work slip, slip, knit, yarn over. The yarn over will become the purl that disappeared when the stitches were worked together. It can also be worked with the decrease after the yarn over: Work to the purl stitch where the yarn over is to be placed, yarn over, knit two together. The yarn over will become the missing purl stitch when worked on the next row.

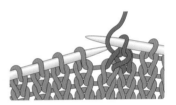

Knit two together, bring yarn over needle.

Larger version: Work to position of buttonhole. Knit two together, yarn over twice, slip, slip, knit, finish the row. On the next row, work a knit and a purl into the double yarn over.

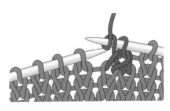

Knit two together, bring yarn over needle twice.

I-CORD-LOOP BUTTONHOLE

THIS TECHNIQUE leaves a virtually invisible loop on the center front, so it will not interrupt a pattern stitch as some of the other buttonholes do. Because it is knit in one piece with the rest of the edging, it is a very strong buttonhole.

Benefits

+ Smoother looking than some of the other buttonholes.
+ Easy to work.
+ Works with all weights of yarn.
+ Will accommodate any size button.
+ Easy to twist large loop into a frog-type closure that can be sewn to the front of the garment.

Drawbacks

+ Takes more time than if pattern were worked without I-cord.
+ Takes more yarn than listed in pattern if pattern does not include I-cord.
+ Thick buttonhole; requires a button with a shank.
+ Easy to make too large. Stays buttoned better if buttonhole has to stretch slightly to go over button.

To Work

For edge with existing stitches: Pick up stitches for front band and work to desired width. With right side facing, cast on three stitches using the cable cast on (see page 14). Work attached I-cord (see page 102) until you reach the area for the buttonhole, then work unattached I-cord as follows: *Knit across the three stitches of I-cord, do not join to center front band. Slip the three stitches just

I-Cord Loop Buttonhole: Existing Stitches

worked back to the left needle as if to purl and repeat from * for desired size loop for button. When the loop is large enough to accommodate the button, resume working attached I-cord to front edge. Repeat for as many buttonholes as needed.

Variation: On the last row of the border for the button band, calculate placement of the buttonholes. When you are knitting the last row and you reach the area for the buttonhole, bind off the stitches for the buttonhole, continue knitting to next buttonhole and repeat. At the end of the row, begin attached I-cord (see page 102). When you reach the bound off areas for the buttonholes, work unattached I-cord to fit over the bound off area.

I-Cord Loop Buttonhole Variation

For edge without stitches: Cast on three stitches and work attached I-cord until you reach the area for the buttonhole. Work unattached I-cord as described at left in "For edge with existing stitches" for desired number of rows for button to fit. Continue with attached I-cord and repeat for each buttonhole.

I-Cord Loop for Edge without Stitches

I-Cord Button Loop to Edge without Stitches

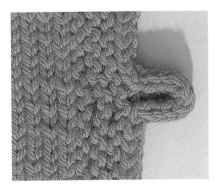

I-Cord Button Loop to Existing Stitches

CROCHET-LOOP BUTTONHOLES

USE THIS technique after all other finishing is complete. There are extra ends to weave in, but they are usually easy to hide in the border.

Benefits
- Easy to add buttonholes that were accidentally left out.
- Easy to add afterthought buttonhole.
- Can be worked with a knit or crochet border in place.
- Loops can be any size needed to accommodate button.
- Works with any stitch pattern in knitting; best used on a firm edge.
- Works well with all weights of yarn.

Drawbacks
- Requires basic crochet skills.
- Leaves a loop on the edge of the knitting.
- Ends must be woven securely or buttonhole may pull apart.

To Work

Mark placement for the buttonholes on the edge of the garment. Use the same number of rows for each buttonhole. Using a crochet hook slightly smaller than the knitting needle used, pull up a loop into the knitting starting at the upper end of the buttonhole. Crochet a chain large enough to accommodate the button. This will decrease in size slightly when you add the second row of cro-

Drop loop off hook.

chet later. Drop the loop off the hook, insert the hook into the knitting at lower end of the buttonhole, place dropped loop back on the hook, yarn over hook and pull it through the knitting. Chain one. Work single crochet over chain, join to knitting at opposite end of buttonhole with a slip stitch. Finish off.

Pull new loop through to connect to knitting.

Single crochet around chain.

Crochet Button Loop to Ribbing

Crochet Button Loop to Garter Stitch

BUTTONHOLE WORKED IN CROCHET BORDER

CROCHET BORDERS on the front edges of a cardigan work well and are very firm. They will keep the edge from rolling and control the curve of the knitting. The buttonhole does not require any additional finishing. It is smooth and almost invisible.

Benefits

- Easy to place buttonhole while working crochet border.
- Works well with all weights of yarn.
- Easy to make for any size button.
- Easy to add an afterthought buttonhole, but requires a single crochet border.

Drawbacks

- Basic crochet skills necessary.
- Easily made too large, and will stretch slightly because it is a vertical buttonhole.

To Work

Mark placement for buttonholes. Use the same number of stitches for each buttonhole. Using a crochet hook two sizes smaller than the knitting needle used to knit the garment, work single crochet for half the number of rows required for the width of the edging. When you reach the area for the buttonhole, work a chain the same number of stitches marked for each buttonhole. Skip the marked area for the buttonhole and continue working single crochet into border. Repeat for each buttonhole. Next row: When you reach the buttonhole chain, work the same number of single crochets around

Crochet Button Hole

the chain as there are stitches in the chain. Repeat for each buttonhole. Work as many rows as desired of single crochet after the buttonholes are completed.

VERTICAL BUTTONHOLE

IN GENERAL, this is the least used of all the buttonholes. It works well in ribbing because it can be hidden between the knit and purl stitches on a horizontal button band that will be sewn on. Because this buttonhole stretches out of shape so easily, it is necessary to reinforce the opening with the buttonhole stitch (see page 126).

Benefits
- Slightly more invisible than horizontal buttonhole.
- Works best in ribbing, but can be used in any other stitch pattern.
- Works well for small buttonholes.
- Works well in horizontal button bands.
- Works best with lighter weight yarns.

Drawbacks
- Stretches out easily, particularly with heavy yarns.
- Requires yarn to be cut and restarted, resulting in added ends to weave in and weakness in area where yarn is restarted.
- Rows must be counted precisely to make both sides of the buttonhole the same length.

To Work

Work to position of buttonhole, place remaining stitches on a holder. Continue knitting until buttonhole is desired length, ending with right-side row (first

side of buttonhole completed). Place the stitches on the holder on another needle and with another piece of yarn, knit to match the length of the first side (second side of buttonhole completed).

Right Half of Vertical Buttonhole
Worked, Left Half on Holder

Rejoin by knitting across first side of buttonhole with main yarn, joining the buttonhole at the top. Leave the ends long enough so that they can be used to reinforce the edge of the buttonhole with buttonhole stitch. Weave in the ends firmly along the edge of the buttonhole to keep the button from stretching the buttonhole.

Top to Bottom:
Vertical Buttonhole in Garter Stitch, Stockinette Stitch, Stockinette Stitch with Garter Stitch at Edge of Buttonhole, Ribbing

BUTTONHOLE STITCH
TO FINISH BUTTONHOLES

THE BUTTONHOLE stitch can be used with any buttonhole to stabilize it, or for decorative purposes on any edge. It should always be used to finish the two-row buttonhole and the vertical buttonhole because they both stretch out of shape easily.

Benefits

♦ Cleans up edge of buttonhole if it is too loose or sloppy looking.

♦ Will make buttonhole smaller if needed.

♦ Works with all weights of yarn; for bulky and worsted-weight yarns, separate the plies to make it less thick when finished.

♦ Can be worked in any yarn for decorative purposes.

Drawbacks

♦ Can easily make the buttonhole look too thick and distort the knitting.

♦ Difficult to work evenly and to make each buttonhole the same size.

♦ Adds more ends to weave in.

To Work

Use the same yarn as was used in the knitting. If yarn is bulky, reduce the thickness by splitting the yarn and using only one or two plies. Starting the yarn at the lower right end of the buttonhole, anchor the tail by going under a stitch on the wrong side of the work, leaving a tail long enough to weave in later. From the right side, insert the needle into the knitting and out the space of the buttonhole, making sure the needle comes out on top of the yarn loop. Continue working toward the left end of the buttonhole, turn knitting, continue across top edge of buttonhole, turn knitting, join to beginning stitch. Weave in ends.

Buttonhole Stitch

Two-Row Buttonhole with
Buttonhole Stitch

ODDS AND ENDS

HERE ARE some tricks and tips that didn't fit into any of the other chapters. They are little things that I think make finishing easier or make the finished garment look or wear better. You'll find that the more finishing you do, the easier it will become, and you might even find some tricks of your own. Write them down; the next time you run across the same finishing problem, you'll know exactly what you did to solve the problem.

Swatching is essential to making your finishing perfect. It is a must, not only for checking the gauge, but for making sure that the pattern stitch looks good in the yarn, finding out whether you need to add a selvage stitch for the pattern, deciding what buttonhole works the best, and so on. If you aren't sure how a technique is going to work out, practice on the swatch; don't work a technique on an entire garment until you're sure it will do what you want it to do. It's frustrating when it doesn't work out and you have to rip out all of your hard work. Buy that extra skein of yarn to use for samples and practice. You'll be happy that you did. Be sure you practice on the same yarn as you knit the garment with; it might not work out the same when you practice on another yarn.

Joining New Yarn
with Knitting in Progress

Always try to join yarn at the beginning of a row. If you are knitting circularly, choose a place that is not in the front of the garment. Imagine where the side seam would be and join it there.

To join the yarn, tie what I call the "magic knot." Tie the new yarn around the old yarn with just a single knot. You'll know you've done it correctly if the knot will slide on the tail of the old yarn. Slide that knot right up to the edge of the knitting, and begin to knit. When you weave your seam, untie the knot.

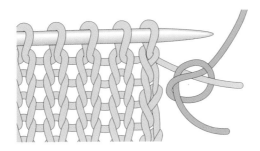

WEAVING IN ENDS

THIS IS the final touch for your garment. Taking the time to do it right will pay off in the finished garment.

♦ When weaving in ends, use a sharp tapestry needle so you can occasionally insert the needle in a strand of yarn in a stitch to hold the ends in place. In wool or blends with fuzzy texture, the yarn end will actually "felt" to the knitting after being worn for a while. This won't happen with cotton.

♦ Do not overcast a seam; it creates too much bulk.

♦ Always try to have all of the ends finish off in a seam, if possible.

Weave ends in through seam in a zig-zag pattern.
(Contrasting yarn for illustration purposes only.)

♦ Weave in an end for about an inch and trim close to the garment.

♦ To weave in the ends from joining new yarn at the selvage edge, untie the "magic knot" twist the yarns, and weave them in the opposite direction.

♦ To weave ends in in the middle of the knitting (though I hope you won't have to do this), cross the yarns to close the little gap and follow the path of a row of horizontal knitting, using the purl bars for 1" or so to weave in the end. Work the other end in the opposite direction.

♦ When working with cotton, the ends won't stay woven in as well as with wools and blends. Weave the end in for more than the inch specified above; in some cases that still won't hold.

- Another way to weave in cotton is to split the ends and weave in two directions, but this gives you double the number of ends to weave in.
- You could also sew down the ends with sewing thread or a light yarn. Securing the ends is especially important in areas that undergo a lot of stretching, like the neck of a crewneck pullover.
- My final advice: Rent an old movie to watch as you finish and weave in the final ends of the garment. A glass of wine wouldn't hurt either.

REINFORCING SHOULDERS

IN COUTURE garments, the shoulders are often reinforced with tape along the shoulder seam. This helps support the weight of the sleeves and keep the shoulders from sagging. In knitted garments, many knitters use crochet to reinforce the shoulders.

To Work

With a crochet hook one to two sizes smaller than the knitting needle used to knit the garment, work a row of slip stitch crochet across the shoulder seam in the same yarn you used to knit the item. It is also good to go across the back neck, especially on a heavy garment. (See "Slip Stitch Crochet," page 104.)

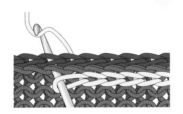

KNITTED SHOULDER PADS

To Work

Using three strands of yarn and a size 11 knitting needle, cast on five stitches. Knit one row. Next row: Increase at the beginning and end of the row. Repeat these two rows in garter stitch until there are approximately twenty-five stitches or until the length down the center equals the width of the shoulder of the sweater. Finish off.

Knit with three strands of worsted-weight yarn on size 11 needles.

Tack the narrow end at the neck edge and the wider end at the sleeve edge. You can adjust the thickness of the shoulder pad by working with fewer or more strands of yarn or a smaller or bigger knitting needle. Knit a small swatch to determine the correct thickness.

Flat Knitting Versus Circular Knitting

Knitting in the round can eliminate a lot of seams, but remember that the more seams a garment has the better it fits. If you are thinking about knitting in the round, consider the points below:

- Requires circular needles of various sizes.
- If the knitting gets twisted when it is joined after the cast-on row, it has to be started over; it cannot be fixed.
- Best method for neckbands and armbands; eliminates a bulky seam.
- Garments knit in the round can twist on the body when worn.
- The stitch gauge must be the same when you are working in the round without purling and when you are working back and forth when dividing for the armholes.
- Must be able to change the pattern stitch from flat to circular.
- Sleeves can be picked up and worked in the round going from the shoulder to the wrist. This requires double-pointed needles as the sleeve gets smaller toward the wrist. The sleeve can also twist around the arm when knit in the round.
- True intarsia cannot be worked in the round.

BLOCKING

OR SHOULD I say "to block or not to block"? The various ways to block a sweater are many, and most people have their favorite. Most knitted garments can use a little smoothing out, or blocking to the correct dimensions. The way you block your garment will have a lot to do with the fiber content of the yarn.

Wool will stand up to any blocking technique as long as it is not steamed so much that the stitches won't bounce back. It will tolerate a little stretch here and there if the garment isn't the right size, too. Blends containing wool and various other fibers will act much the same as wool.

Acrylic is better blocked with a damp towel. Steam will take the life out of the stitches, and if you use an iron and the iron touches the garment, it will smash the knitting and never come back to its original state.

Cottons do well with the damp-towel technique. Or you can dampen a cotton sweater and place it in the dryer for a brief time. I find when I wash a cotton sweater that if I put it in the dryer and dry slightly, it goes right back to its original size. I then lay it flat to continue drying.

Where to Block Your Garment

You will need a flat surface where you can leave the damp knitting until it is dry. The surface will need to take pins if you are doing pin blocking. The top of a bed (without an electric blanket) or a blocking board work well. The floor covered with a sheet or a piece of fabric, where no one will walk (and the cat and the dog won't run across) is also a good place. An ironing board will work for small pieces that fit exactly on the top without falling over the edges. In cold, damp climates the drying process could take a long time, so you might want to set up a fan or portable heater so the piece dries before it begins to mildew or smell musty.

The Damp-Towel Technique

Lay out the pieces of the garment and lay a damp towel over them for an hour or two. Do not saturate the towel with water, but wet it lightly or spray it with water. Remove the towel, leaving the pieces damp enough to shape into the correct dimensions. You can pin the edges or just shape the pieces. Smooth with your hand. Leave to dry. Be sure the side seams of the front and back are the same length. You can also use this technique on a completed garment to "freshen" it or take away baggy elbows.

Pin Blocking

With measurements of the knitted pieces in hand, a spray bottle, and lots of T-pins that won't rust, lay out the pieces, right side up. Begin pinning out the width and the length to match the measurements given in the pattern. Pin out the entire piece, except for the ribbing if it is to pull in slightly. Mist heavily with water, and allow to dry before removing.

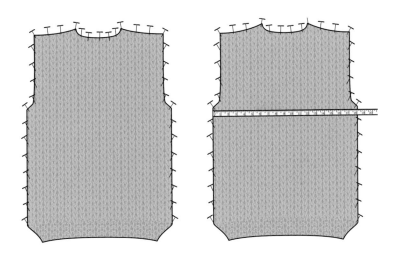

Steaming Method

Pin out the pieces exactly as you would in the pin-blocking method. With a hot iron set on steam, gently move the iron over the knitted pieces. Do not allow the iron to touch the knitting; it will flatten the knitting and sometimes leave a little shine on the yarn. Use a thin towel over the piece to prevent accidentally touching the knitting. The towel could be damp to make more steam. Do not remove knitting until completely dry.

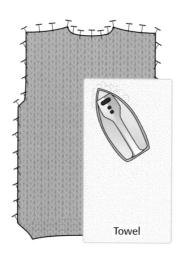

Towel

SWEATER AND YARN STORAGE

AFTER YOU'VE completed your knitting, store the piece safely. That is, keep it where the moths won't get it, the sun won't fade it, and its shape will remain the same. Careful storage isn't difficult, but it does take some time and effort. All of the tips below apply to yarn storage as well.

Moths

First of all, it isn't every moth that eats sweaters. The average everyday flying moth is not what eats your sweater. It is only the clothes moth. Clothes moths lay their eggs on your garment. When the eggs hatch, they eat their way to life by dining on your sweater, generally on the front. The reason for this is that microscopic drops of food or oil land on the front of the sweater while you're eating or cooking. You don't know they're there, but the moths will find them. They love to lay their eggs in those tasty spots.

To prevent moth damage:

+ Never store something that is dirty. I don't mean dragged through the mud; I mean worn a few times. Too often, when the weather changes, garments get put away before they are cleaned.
+ Moths hate sunlight. If possible, don't store your garments in the dark.
+ If you use plastic bags, be sure the garment is completely dry before putting it in the airtight bag. Moisture will invite mildew. You can prick the bag with a pin in a few spots to allow the sweater to "breathe," thus preventing mildew. Do this with your stash of yarn as well. Don't put the yarn away in the bag from the store; treat it as you would treat a sweater.
+ Finally, cedar chests and cedar blocks will not guarantee you won't have moths for forever. Cedar should be oiled or sanded to renew the smell at least every couple of years or so. You can also keep moths away by fooling them with different smells. Place bay leaves, potpourri, or scented oil along with the cedar. Be sure the oil isn't touching the sweaters. These scents will fool moths. Moths get resistant to cedar after it begins to lose its smell. A new smell will confuse them, and they will go elsewhere.

Final Tips

+ Fold sweaters; don't hang them.
+ If you hand wash, be sure the sweater has a warm place to dry. If the sweater has to sit for days to dry, it will begin to smell like mildew. Use a space heater or fan if necessary to keep the air moving around the sweater.
+ Do not dry clean cotton sweaters. The dry-cleaning process will make them larger.

WORKSHEET I

PLANNING YOUR KNITTING AND FINISHING

*I*F YOU are using a commercial pattern, read through the directions to see if they tell you what type of cast on, increases, or decreases to use. Most of them won't, so you'll be on your own to figure that out. If you're designing your own garment, you will also need to consider all of these options.

The worksheet opposite is designed to help you decide what techniques you are going to use, so that when the garment is finished everything will match and you won't have any surprises.

IT'S ESSENTIAL to write things down. If you have to put the knitting away for awhile and you don't remember what you did or what needle you used, you'll find it very frustrating. If you work on more than one project at a time, it is even more critical to keep separate notes of each. I have a friend who writes on scraps of paper. It works for her, as long as she doesn't lose them and keeps them in order.

I keep a notebook where I knit and constantly make notes about things I am doing, especially when the pattern has to be written later. Believe me, once I've finished a garment and moved on to the next design, I won't remember how I did a "special" thing. This isn't an age thing; it's just the way it is. Another motivation for keeping notes is that you might want to use something really nifty you created on one sweater on another sweater at a later time. If you've written it down, you won't have to figure it out again; you can just go back in your notebook and find what you did.

Body needle size _____ Number of skeins of yarn _____

Border needle size _____

Stitch gauge _____

Row gauge _____

Type of cast on _____

Type of border; rib or other stitch pattern _____

Number of rows _____ to equal _____ inch(es)

Selvage stitch(es)? _____

Type of increases above ribbing if any (body and sleeve)

_____

Increase used for sleeve shaping _____

Number of rows to armholes _____

Type of sleeve opening _____

Shaping: Decreases on the edge or full fashion? _____

Number of rows in sleeve opening _____

Shoulders: Type of seam _____

Short rows on shoulders? _____

Front bands, if any, knit on or sewn on later? _____

Buttonholes, what type? _____

How many stitches to pick up or rows to knit _____

Neckband, what type? _____

Number of stitches to pick up _____

Armband (if there is one), what type? _____

Number of stitches to pick up _____

Type of bind off to match cast on _____

WORKSHEET II

DETERMINING INCREASE, DECREASE, AND BUTTONHOLE PLACEMENT

OME SIMPLE math is required to figure out where to place increases, decreases, and buttonholes so they have the same number of stitches or rows between them. The following example will show you how to calculate buttonhole placement. The method is the same for calculating increases and decreases. There is a worksheet to simplify the math, but the following paragraphs will help you understand what you are doing.

To calculate buttonhole placement, count the number of rows or stitches to be used for the entire buttonhole band. Let's say the front bands will require 120 rows of knitting. At this point you must choose which buttonhole you are going to use. I'll use the 2-row buttonhole for this example. There will be 7 buttonholes. If we are placing 7 buttonholes and they each take 2 rows, 2 rows times 7 buttonholes equals 14 rows. Subtract the 14 rows from the total rows of 120 to equal 106 rows.

Now calculate how many rows or stitches there will be between the buttonholes. The buttonholes should not be located too close to the bottom or the top. Let's say we want the first buttonhole to be 6 rows from the bottom and the last buttonhole 6 rows from the top. Subtract these 12 rows from the 106 rows to equal 94 rows left to divide evenly between the buttonholes. If we are placing 7 buttonholes, there are 6 spaces between them. Divide 94 rows by 6 spaces to equal 15 rows between buttonholes, plus a fraction, which means there are extra rows. To determine how many extra rows there are, multiply 15 rows times 6 spaces to equal 90. Then subtract 90 rows from 94 rows to get 4 extra rows that need to be placed somewhere. We can place 2 at the bottom and 2 at the top, but it would be better if all buttonholes are made on the right-side row so they look the same. For that to happen there has to be an even number of rows between the buttonholes. So we could add one of the 4 extra rows to 4 of the spaces between the buttonholes, but that leaves 2 spaces with 15 rows. Instead, take 2 rows from below the bottom buttonhole or above the top buttonhole and place one in each of the 2 spaces that have only 15 rows between the buttonholes to make all buttonholes occur every 16 rows. Don't take 1 row from each end, because that will place the buttonhole on a wrong-side row, which is what we are trying to avoid.

Use the following worksheet to help you calculate the number of rows (or stitches) to place between increases, decreases, or buttonholes.

Number of rows (or stitches)   _____ (A)

Number of rows (or stitches)
to work one inc, dec, or buttonhole   _____ (B)

Total number of inc, dec, or buttonholes   _____ (C)

Multiply B times C   = _____ (D)

Subtract D from A   = _____ (E)

Number of rows (or stitches) before
first inc, dec, or buttonhole, and after last
inc, dec, or buttonhole   _____ (F)

Subtract F from E   = _____ (G) total number of rows (or
stitches) to place between inc, dec,
or buttonholes

Divide G by the number of spaces between
inc, dec, or buttonholes

$G \div$ _____ = _____(H) number of
rows (or stitches) between inc, dec, or
buttonholes. If there is a fraction, see
next steps.

If there is a remainder, place extra
stitches at beginning or end,
or between inc, dec, or buttonholes   _____(I) total number of rows
(or stitches) between inc,
dec, or buttonholes

Multiply H times number of spaces
between inc, dec, or buttonholes

$H \times$ _____ = _____(I) number of
rows (or stitches) used between inc, dec,
or buttonholes

Then subtract I from G $G - I =$ _____(J) extra rows (or stitches)
that need to be placed somewhere; refer
to text for placing rows or stitches

RESOURCES

Bryson Distributing
4065 West 11th Avenue #39
Eugene, OR 97402

Knitter's safety pins (safety pins without the loop that acts as a spring at the coiled end of a standard safety pin. They are used in knitting because they don't catch in the yarn.)

Cascade Yarns
1224 Andover Park East
Tukwila, WA 98188

All yarn used in the book: Cascade 220 knit on size 5 for ribbing and size 7 for everything else, except shoulder pad (see instructions on page 132).

BIBLIOGRAPHY

Buller, Kate. *The Ultimate Knitter's Guide.* Bothell, Wash.: Martingale & Company, 2000.

Hiatt, June. *The Principles of Knitting.* New York: Simon and Schuster, 1988.

Wiseman, Nancie M. *Knitted Shawls, Stoles, and Scarves.* Bothell, Wash.: Martingale and Company, 2001.

————. *Knitted Sweaters for Every Season.* Bothell, Wash.: Martingale & Company, 2002.

Vogue Knitting. New York: Pantheon Books, 1989.

ABOUT THE AUTHOR

While working as a registered nurse in 1987, Nancie opened a yarn shop, Nancie Knits, in Sacramento, California. While running the store, Nancie began to teach classes locally and nationwide. Teaching led to the start of her video-production company, Wisewater Productions, and the success of seven knitting videos to date.

Nancie has written patterns and designed for *Interweave Knits, Knitter's Magazine,* and *Piecework Magazine.* In the fall of 1997, Nancie was the consultant for "Knitting 101," an article in *Martha Stewart Living.*

Nancie's first book, *Lace from the Attic,* started her on a path of historical research into all types of lace, including tatting, crochet, and bobbin lace. Her second book was *Knitted Shawls, Stoles, and Scarves* (Martingale & Company, 2001). *Knitted Sweaters for Every Season* (Martingale & Company, 2002), Nancie's third book, was based on the techniques in the shawl book.

Nancie lives in Coupeville, Washington, with her husband, Bill Attwater, and their two dogs, Christina and Amber.

INDEX